GREAT M
IN AVI
an
ORANGES
THE ONLY FRUIT

Directed by Beeban Kidron and produced by Phillippa Giles *Great Moments in Aviation* stars Vanessa Redgrave, John Hurt, Jonathan Pryce, Dorothy Tutin and introduces Rakie Ayola as Gabriel Angel. *Great Moments in Aviation* will have cinematic release in the Spring 1994 and will be screened by the BBC in 1995.

Jeanette Winterson's adaptation of her first novel, *Oranges Are Not the Only Fruit*, was an internationally acclaimed television drama awarded a *BAFTA* for best drama and an *RTS* award in the same year; the *Prix Italia; FIPA D'Argent* at Cannes for best script, *The Golden Gate* in San Francisco and an *ACE* Award at the Los Angeles television festival.

Jeanette Winterson's most recent novel is *Art & Lies*. She is also the author of *Written on the Body*, a love story; *Sexing the Cherry*, winner of the E. M. Forster Award from the American Academy for Arts and Letters; and *The Passion*, winner of the 1987 John Llewellyn Rhys Prize.

Jeanette Winterson

GREAT MOMENTS IN AVIATION

and

ORANGES ARE NOT THE ONLY FRUIT

Two Filmscripts

VINTAGE

First published in Vintage 1994

1 3 5 7 9 10 8 6 4 2

GREAT MOMENTS IN AVIATION
first published by Vintage, 1994

© Jeanette Winterson 1994

ORANGES ARE NOT THE ONLY FRUIT
first published by Pandora Press, 1990
Vintage edition 1994

© Jeanette Winterson 1990

Vintage Books
Random House UK Ltd, 20 Vauxhall Bridge Road, London SW1V 2SA

Random House Australia (Pty) Limited
20 Alfred Street, Milsons Point, Sydney,
New South Wales 2061, Australia

Random House New Zealand Limited
18 Poland Road, Glenfield
Auckland 10, New Zealand

Random House South Africa (Pty) Limited
PO Box 337, Bergvlei, South Africa

Random House UK Limited Reg. No. 954009

ISBN 0 09 928541 X

Typeset by Deltatype Ltd, Ellesmere Port, Cheshire
Printed and bound in Great Britain by
Cox & Wyman Ltd, Reading, Berkshire

CONTENTS

INTRODUCTION

Great Moments in Aviation is not a film about aeroplanes. In the old days, when it first came out, *Oranges Are Not the Only Fruit* used to appear on the cookery shelves of mainstream bookshops. I am hoping that the intervening years and a well-known reputation for loosening words from the grip of a single meaning, will save me from the rage of plane buffs across the world.

Although *Great Moments in Aviation* is not about aeroplanes, it is about powered flight, the flight of the imagination. Only by imagining what we might be can we become more than we are. That is the talisman of the film.

My work is always concerned with journeys; the space travelled, physical and metaphysical, between two points of beginning. There are no endings, there are pauses, rests, redirections, revelations, but the journey continues, even for those who are convinced that the only important thing is to get from A to B.

THE BEGINNING

Great Moments in Aviation came out of a series of conversations with a close friend, the black actress, Vicky Licorish. I felt that the mundane facts of so many emigration stories could lead to a world of infinite possibility. Of course, the dream itself, the dream which pushes so many people to uproot everything, is one of infinite possibility. For better or for worse, the emigrant believes that the Promised Land exists.

I took as my starting part the idea of a journey borne out of hope. A hope, so fierce and bright that it would outshine many more sophisticated qualities, like worldly wisdom and even self-knowledge. My heroine, Gabriel Angel is full of hope and it is through her agency that the rather tired, fleeting world of the everyday, is transformed into something more optimistic and valuable.

THE SCRIPT

My interest in working for film and television is inevitably evangelical. I have a mission and it is this: to restore to the image the power of the word. Film is not painting, it cannot satisfactorily exist without language but it mistakes the debased language of daily contact with the language of art. Do not misunderstand me here, the language of art is not far removed from the language of conversation, it shares the same raw material but it is subtly elaborated to remove what is banal and to include what is poetic. This is generally achieved through word order within the sentences and through the structure of those sentences when placed side by side. The words themselves must be carefully chosen to avoid that 'worn-out' feeling that accompanies so much awful prose, awful poetry and awful script-writing. In cinema there are too many absurd situations where an art film of great visual originality tows a script that is banal. The redundancy of the language dilutes the strength of the whole. Very often an audience is dissatisfied not by what they see but by what they hear. Sadly, the film world itself is largely indifferent to the possibilities of language and therefore encourages an environment where weak scripts are likely to be the only scripts. It is quite wrong to assume that a good director and good actors need nothing more than a coherent plot and something to talk about. That is not script. Hollywood thinks it is and since there is no British film industry, good writers here are in deep trouble.

In any film that is trying to do something difficult, controversial or new, it is essential that the script first and foremost should identify and meet those challenges. A weak script cannot be redeemed by any amount of directorial or actorial charisma. A weak script is one where language is not an end in itself but only a means to an end. A trolley to convey information, a slop-bucket to carry the emotional interest. Where language is always treated like a servant, it will not have any glory to show. I don't want to give orders to a servant, I prefer, like Jacob, to wrestle with an angel.

A great deal of wrestling went into *Great Moments in Aviation*. The film is always working on two levels, the outer experience of the journey with its rather frightening ramifications, and the inner experiences of the characters, experiences which will change all of them forever. Obviously these levels interweave as the film gains ground but part of the dramatic tension is to keep separating them, so that there is a clash of order between the inner and outer worlds, a clash that cannot be resolved by commonsense but only through love. There is then, a satisfying plot in the old fashioned way, although I have not structured it in an old-fashioned way. That had to be watched carefully as the film's metaphysics developed. It is so easy to lose the balance of a script and although too many films sacrifice too much for plot, it is just as annoying when an art film loses its pace in meaningless musicality. I didn't want to lock up this film in art-house, but nor did I want to busy myself with up-market entertainment. Can a balance be struck? Yes and no. Emphatically films are a compromise. They cost too much and they involve large numbers of people some of them with impossibly conflicting interests. What begins as virgin territory, the script, safe and private in the writer's hands, soon becomes a polygamous marriage. We all lay claim and we all believe our claim is the right one. I have had to lose some things I valued, some wonderfully witty lines, and an emphasis on the inner life. Perhaps it was an over-emphasis but I shall never know because I shall never see that other film. This is curious. As a fiction writer I am at liberty to make two versions of the same piece although only one will ever be public. I can travel down the unseen road. In film that is not possible and I do not see how either the writer or the director can avoid being haunted by ghosts. So much for speculation. There is one film, one script and one compromise I will not make, not now not ever. That is a compromise over the *structure* of the film. A structure which is integral to a strong script and which cannot be given away without making a totally different film. The structure of a film should not be accidental. Its order should not be just one way among many of conveying information and emotion. There is a huge difference between a work that is structured and a work that is simply arranged. *Great Moments in Aviation* is not an arrangement of scenes like beads on a string, it had to be made as a whole, not as a flexible number of interconnecting parts. If anyone is confused by the notion of structure, it might help to think of the film geometrically. The film has a particular shape, just as a triangle say, has a particular shape. Whilst it is possible to work with points on the line of the triangle, just as it is possible to work with individual moments in the film, it is not possible to tinker with the structure without misshaping the whole. Film is a tinkering sort of business and unless a writer can defend the structure of the script, and that means knowing exactly why it is what it is, somebody else will get out the maniacal socket set and take it apart.

Am I talking about integrity of vision? Yes, but vision can only be realised through form. Musicians and painters know that, people who work with words very often do not. The bad writer, and that includes most writers, mistakes the content for the form. The bad writer assumes that what is said is more important than how it is said. Sincerity of emotion is not enough. In art only sincerity of form is enough. It is *through* the form, not in spite of it or accidental to it, that the most powerful emotions are let loose over the greatest number of people. That is why, in film above all, where interference is normal, the scriptwriter must joint and plane her work into a shape that is not only satisfying but also authentic to itself. The point is not that the script should overbalance the film but that it should not disappear inside it. A script is more than a plot, a guide-line, a story, a set of characters, it is the language it uses. That language makes a particular shape, a shape which should inform and excite the images used. It is language and image, image and language, working fully together that create the best films.

NOTIONS OF FAIRYTALE

I am not interested in Realism for its own sake. It is not self-justifying, although it is assumed to be so. There are a number of narrative devices of which Realism is only one. It is important to remember that Realism is a device and not a place. A fiction is a fiction no matter where or when or how it is set. The point of fiction is not to mirror real life but to set out from it, to alter our viewing angle and perhaps even the world we are viewing.

Great Moments in Aviation uses an opening sequence designed to draw the audience out of the world of their own concerns and into a world whose customs are strange. In the new world, objects are unfamiliar and events do not follow the usual rules. The coincidence of colour and language, each more vivid than normal, pull the viewer forward with fairytale immediacy. We find ourselves in Gabriel's world, a world which holds good throughout the film. We are getting more than information, more than emotion, the beginning is the touchstone for the entire piece.

The confidence of fairytale has always pleased me. With admirable economy and sure-footedness, the fairytale starts straight in with what is essential. There is no preamble, no tedious family trees, no maundering introduction of the *dramatis personae*. We go to the heart and we stay there. Fairytale is the antidote to Realist padding. There is so little we need to know. I wanted a script that could use the conventions of the fairytale without losing emotional depth (which fairytales don't have) and without losing all contact with the world as we know it. It was right then to set the film on a boat, a sealed and concealed world with its own identity and rituals, at once both recognisable and odd. Fairytale never leaves the reader in a familiar spot, we are whisked away to a wood or a lake or a castle or an island, each a law unto itself made all the more uncomfortable because it isn't as weird as, say, planet Mars. We think we will be able to cope just by using our usual tool kit, how disconcerting it is when we can't.

NOTIONS OF PLOT

Plot bothers me. I do not like it. I think it is best left to crime writers of the old school. Unfortunately cinema has chosen to follow a novelistic rather than a theatric tradition. Worse, it has chosen to follow a novelistic tradition that was already out of date when cinema began. The nineteenth century is a curious place for that vast battery of technical achievement to make its home. Film technology is now much more sophisticated than film experiment. Film could do anything but what does it like to do best? Tell stories in the old-fashioned way.

I admire Peter Greenaway and Derek Jarman because they have refused the filmic legacy and continued to work as soldiers of fortune. Their film-making is European not American, certainly not British, if we look at the sort of thing Britain made when she had an industry rather than a hobby. The American death-grip is so pervasive that it has strangled an alternative history for film which includes all the great film-makers, Buñuel, Fellini, Bergman (you know the list), giving out the lie that what ought to be the real current of film-making is only the ebb and flow of art-house eccentrics. Great but not popular, genius but tedious. Hollywood's obsession with plot, with stars, with glitter and noise had disguised the true potential of film-making. The emphasis on money has made it virtually impossible to do anything if they won't pay for it. There are always exceptions, thank God there are, but far fewer exceptions to the Hollywood rule than at any other time in film.

What do I do? Compromise. In order to raise the money for this film, and about one quarter of it had to come from America, the burden of plot had to be shouldered. It is a good plot if you like plot and if you don't it is at least always leading inwards, away from itself towards more challenging emotional and spiritual questions. That is the best I could do.

CHARACTER

Again I wanted to follow the fairytale convention. A heroine, a hero, a villain and a fairy godmother. As you would expect, I have reworked those archetypes quite a lot but there is still an archetypal resonance to the characters which gives an underlying coherence to themselves as individuals and as reactors upon each other.

Gabriel Angel is the heroine, a black woman coming to England in the late fifties, to follow a dream. On board ship she meets Duncan Stewart, a Scot and not a Scot, a forger, a fantasist, a most compelling man. Rex Goodyear, art expert and obsessive, is not a typical villain, he may not be a villain at all, it is difficult not to pity him even at his vilest.

Miss Bead and Miss Quim. Why have one fairy godmother when you could have two? Retired missionaries on their way home to England after thirty years in the service of the Lord. They are in love and not in love.

The spread of the characters in terms of sex, sexuality, class, race and culture gave me enormous scope. I was able to use the paradox of concentrating the film very tightly on their lives while spreading out considerably in terms of ideas. The film is at once focussed and diffuse. The camera takes the same liberty giving a film of claustrophobic power and great freedom. The characters are decidedly not the sort of people you are likely to meet in the street, they are not the sort of people sitting in the audience. In spite of that difference there is an intimacy between viewer and viewed, an identification of dreams. The dreams on board ship are worth having, the characters who embody those dreams are worth loving. Even Rex Goodyear is worthy of pity. I wanted the audience to come away with something valuable, the talisman I talked of earlier, I believe that they do.

The characters, Duncan, Gabriel, Miss Bead and Miss Quim, all find something of value where they least expected it, Rex Goodyear finds that the things we value are very often worthless.

THE FILM

And the ghosts of those other films. I do not feel, as I did with the TV version of *Oranges Are Not the Only Fruit*, that *Great Moments in Aviation* is the definitive film. I do not see how we could have done *Oranges* better, I do see how we could have done *Great Moments* better. That may be because I am more conscious than I was, more aware of possibilities and pitfalls, or it may be that the sheer scale of film as opposed to TV makes too much compromise inevitable.

The trouble is that I don't care what people think of my work I only care about doing my work to the best of my ability. I am ruthless with myself, far more ruthless than any critic has ever been and rather more intelligent too. If I am satisfied that is enough. I am not easy to satisfy.

Having made that statement, anyone who has worked with me will also say that I am happy to make cuts and changes when those cuts and changes demonstrably benefit the whole. Nothing is sacred, everything is open to question, but once those questions have been answered only someone with a confidence problem will be prepared to change their minds under further pressure. In film there is always further pressure. It seems to me that if the director, the writer and the producer have agreed that should be the end of the matter. I have discovered that it is only the beginning of the matter. The power of the marketing men, the distributors, the festival organizers, the award pundits, is enormous. The power of the people not making the film is at least as great as the power of those who are.

Every picture tells a story. There are more stories to the making of *Great Moments* than I would care to tell but there is one story that I can tell in order to get to the end; the end of the film, the end of the script, the end of this introduction, and to the beginning of another story, another film.

Imagine a man of Old Testament dimensions; a patriarch who has heard of feminism, a bully who knows the tender touch, a now and again visionary who can see beyond media America but mostly won't. A man who has made wonderful things and dreadful things. A man who will get behind a project even if it means pushing it over a cliff. An emotional man whose name is Terrible Tough Guy. Imagine Harvey Weinstein.

Harvey Weinstein runs Miramax and Miramax was behind *Cinema Paradiso, Like Water For Chocolate, Paris is Burning . . .* and *Great Moments in Aviation*. Our American friends who put up 25% of the money and insisted that we re-work the end before the film could be released.

I think that Harvey was right about the end and wrong about the solution. That argument took us all the best part of a year and was finally resolved in 1994 when Beeban took another $200,000 and a crew to the Caribbean. I sent a couple of pages of script. Probably the most expensive words I will ever write, unless of course I get caught up with Harvey again, and both of us being a pair of scrappers, I probably will.

The new ending is satisfying and it fits with the re-cut of the film. I think that the film has lost some of the dimensions that were important to me but it has gained a pacey and well balanced very filmic sense.

It is a good movie but it is not the movie I thought we could make. Obviously that raises a lot of difficult questions for me, I do not want to make compromises, even when they turn out to be stylish and enjoyable compromises. I do like *Great Moments in Aviation* but there is another film there somewhere that has got lost.

I am coming back to the idea that made me chary of film-work a long time ago. The idea that something of significance can only come out of a single vision, a single mind, single control. Those films which seem to me to be most important are the work of a director who is not contending with anything other than a subordinate screen-writer, if indeed he or she has not worked the script themselves from the start. Visions clash, no doubt about it, and the film that Beeban wanted, and the film that Harvey wanted, were two entirely separate films from the film I wanted. In the end, we have got a film we all like, but is that enough? Not enough for me.

I struggle. I love the possibilities of the wide screen and I know that the screen needs language as desperately as it needs true images. How to resolve this? I will have to deal with those failures that were entirely my own within *Great Moments in Aviation*, the gaps where I left too much to the imagination, because of course, a fiction writer glories in gaps, cinema hates them. I will have to recognise that there are routes I cannot take on screen, and find other cunning passes to get round the demands of the production and the director's lens. A lot of directors think they want to work with me but that is because they think they want a superior script. But do they? A superior script can't come out of a hack mentality but a hack mentality is necessary to a director who wants control. I don't blame the director but director and writer in search of excellence need to recognise a fundamental fight that may only end in tears. I think the risk is worth it but, as yet, I do not know that it is worth it. That's another story, or do I mean another film?

Jeanette Winterson
London 1994.

Great Moments in Aviation

CAST

GABRIEL ANGEL	A black woman, early twenties.
DUNCAN STEWART	A Scot and not a Scot. Thirties or early forties. Handsome.
REX GOODYEAR	An art dealer. Fifties.
DOCTOR BEAD	A missionary, just retired. Tall and stately. Sixties.
MISS QUIM	A missionary, just retired. Stocky and robust. Sixties.
VESUVIA	Gabriel's Grandmother. Chiselled and wise. Age uncertain.
THOMAS	Gabriel's Grandfather. Grisled and jolly. Age uncertain.
MICHAEL	Gabriel's husband. Young and attractive.
AMERICAN WOMAN	A passenger.

STEWARDS AND VARIOUS CREW MEMBERS, STAFF AND GUESTS

The action takes place on board on ocean-going Cruise Ship inside and out. Also in Vesuvia's hut and on the dockside. FLASHBACKS are mostly aeroplanes, runways and beaches.

1. INT. CARIBBEAN HUT. NIGHT 1

A long, low hut in the Caribbean.

The room is simply furnished but a long trestle table is set for dinner, dominates the scene. In the centre of the table is a huge silver tureen covered with a lid.

Sitting around the table are NINE BLACK GUESTS *of different sexes, an old black matriarch,* VESUVIA, *and her grand-daughter* GABRIEL ANGEL, *a young woman of about twenty-five.*

VESUVIA *is at the head of the table,* GABRIEL, *at the foot. Both are finely dressed in a homespun way.*

Here is a feast, opulence, lots of food and floral decorations.

An open fire, eerie and primitive burns at the back of the room. Flares light the room.

Time and trouble, rather than money have been spent.

VESUVIA *stands up and bangs the table with a mallet.*

VESUVIA: Quiet now. Quiet. Give a moment to Vesuvia. Every year we gather here to keep the memory of my husband, Thomas. You all knew him as a magician, and entertainer, a man of the air. Nine years ago when he was flying that old mail plane, he vanished. We don't know where his body came to rest, but his heart was always where it should have been and his spirit is with us here tonight.

[VESUVIA *gestures towards the empty place at the table. The* GUESTS *nod.*]

VESUVIA: Tonight, there's another reason for our gathering. Not death but life. My grand-daughter Gabriel is setting out on a journey to find her fortune. Just like her Grand-daddy Thomas, she says she knows it's out there somewhere. [VESUVIA *laughs*] It sure ain't here. Gabriel's going to England to join her husband Michael. His hard work has sent her the money for the passage but it's his love that's truly taking her there.

[*Murmurs of approval from the* GUESTS.]

3

[GABRIEL *looks down at the table.*]

VESUVIA: You all know the story of the pot of gold at the end of the rainbow. It was Grand-daddy Thomas who said 'Gabriel, you can walk all day just to find the rainbow's already gone, or you can get your feet off the ground and *fly* into that rainbow.' Come forward now, each one of you, and with your hearts and with your hands, give Gabriel the blessings she needs for her journey. Our journey.

[*The* GUESTS *come forward to* GABRIEL, *touch her and offer their blessing.*]

FIRST GUEST: I touch you with money for all your needs.

SECOND GUEST: I touch you with health for all your days.

THIRD GUEST: I touch you with laughter for all your woes.

FOURTH GUEST: I touch you with pleasure for all your nights.

FIFTH GUEST: I touch you with children for your old age.

SIXTH GUEST: I touch you with strength for all you must do.

SEVENTH GUEST: I touch you with wisdom for all you must say.

EIGHTH GUEST: I touch you with food for your belly.

NINTH GUEST: I touch you with a roof and four square walls.

[VESUVIA *comes forward and takes* GABRIEL's *hands.*]

VESUVIA: I touch you for us all. Those of us here, those of us gone. [*She touches* GABRIEL's *belly*] I touch you with my courage and your Grand-daddy's dreams.

[VESUVIA *motions the* GUESTS *back to the table one by one, as they give their blessings.*]

[*When all are seated again, she focuses our attention on a large silver platter covered with a lid. She lifts up the lid, slowly, slowly. Resting on the platter is a perfect model of a hot air balloon.*]

VESUVIA: It was in the year 1703, in the country of Portugal, that Father Bartolomeu came up with the idea of flying. He liked to think of the angels with their great gold wings cut across the sun and their bodies bright as dragonflies.

[*She lights a fierce-looking taper and moves it towards the balloon. We see that there are two little people in the basket. She lights the gas chamber. The balloon hesitates and gently lifts off towards the ceiling.*]

2. EXT. QUAYSIDE. DAY 2. DAWN

All we see throughout this montage are parts of the body:

Hands loading luggage onto a steep conveyor belt: trunks, packing cases, suitcases, a rail of stewards' uniforms [white jackets trimmed with gold, quasi military effect], baskets overflowing with vegetables.

An elephant carrying a rich gold cabin trunk sways up the gang-plank.

Arms thick and hairy, black and white, hoisting and loading.

Feet: bare feet, brogue shod feet, shiny men's knee boots, women's feet in cuban heels.

Hoofs, paws, jostling and bustling with the feet around great coils of rope and dockside trappings.

Torsos: the gleaming sweating upper bodies of bearers carrying baskets of meat and fish on their heads, some balance bolts of brightly coloured cloth, one has a gaudy parrot on each shoulder.

Mouths crying out, buying and selling. White teeth, broken teeth.

We see various members of the CAST *embarking.*

Into this melee, in full shot from head to foot, GABRIEL *and* VESUVIA *hugging one another.*

The ship hoots. Clangs its bell.

Through this rushing and roaring, the still point of the turning world, GABRIEL *and* VESUVIA, *their faces. This is goodbye.*

3. EXT. DECK. DAY 2

GABRIEL *crosses the ship's deck, pushing through* GROUPS OF PEOPLE *chattering and organising themselves. They are all white.*

She's carrying a little suitcase and a piece of paper. She keeps glancing at the paper. She arrives at a staircase going below. It's marked 'D'. She checks her paper again. We see it's a line map of the deck with 'D' marked in red.

4. INT. STAIRS & D22 CORRIDOR. DAY 2

She goes down the narrow stairs, which end at a corridor lined with cabin doors.

At the far end of the corridor is another set of stairs leading back to the deck.

GABRIEL *opens the door of cabin D22.*

5. INT. CABIN D22. DAY 2

Two bunks. A dressing table. Small writing table. Two chairs. A fifties travel poster advertising the joys of going by liner.

GABRIEL *pushes her little suitcase onto the top bunk, checks her lipstick in the mirror, and goes out of the cabin.*

6. INT. CORRIDOR OUTSIDE D22. DAY 2

GABRIEL *goes up the same stairs she came down.*

As her legs disappear, we see another pair of legs coming down the opposite stairs. A man's legs, in a kilt. He's carrying luggage and a set of bagpipes. He checks his bit of paper and goes into D22.

7. INT. CABIN D22. DAY 2

The MAN *dumps his stuff in a messy boy's way and doesn't notice Gabriel's neat little suitcase on the top bunk.*

He gets out a whisky bottle from the pouch of his bagpipes, a collapsible cup from his sporran and pours a generous swig. He toasts himself in the dressing-table mirror, then downs the glass in one, and starts taking off his clothes.

The MAN *is stripped to the waist and dealing with the pin of his kilt, when* GABRIEL *returns, holding a large black umbrella.*

She looks taken aback.

DUNCAN *is unperturbed. He glances at her.*

DUNCAN: Hello, I'm glad to see you, although, it's always a good idea to knock. Hang my clothes will you?

[DUNCAN *gestures towards his heap on the bed and gets out of his kilt.*]

[DUNCAN'*s now in underpants, socks and brogues. He turns his back to* GABRIEL *and fishes out a shirt from his overflowing suitcase.*]

GABRIEL: This is my cabin.

[DUNCAN *wheels round and stares at her.*]

[*She points with her brolly to her neat little suitcase.*]

GABRIEL: That's my suitcase.

[DUNCAN *has his shirt on, but unfastened. He grabs the nearest thing to hand* [*his bagpipes*] *to hold up against his lower body.*]

DUNCAN: I thought you were the . . .

[GABRIEL *raises her eyebrows at him.*]

[*He daren't say 'maid'. He reaches into the sporran of his kilt and pulls out a cabin list.*]

[GABRIEL *takes hers from her hangbag.*]

DUNCAN: D22?

GABRIEL: D22.

[*They read in unison from their respective lists. But* DUNCAN *says 'Mr' before both his name and Gabriel's.*]

DUNCAN: D22. Mr Gabriel Angel and Mr Duncan Stewart.

GABRIEL: Miss Gabriel Angel and Miss D. Stewart.

[GABRIEL *and* DUNCAN *glare at one another.*]

[DUNCAN *starts fastening his shirt with one hand, holding up his bagpipes with the other.*]

DUNCAN: Well, I'm *Mr* Duncan Stewart.

GABRIEL: And I'm *Miss* Gabriel Angel.

DUNCAN: You're supposed to be a man.

GABRIEL: You're supposed to be a woman.

[*They both look at his kilt.*]

DUNCAN: Yes, well, I'm not. [*he pauses*] Would you mind passing me those trousers please?

[GABRIEL *fishes up the trousers on the tip of her umbrella and swings them over to* DUNCAN.]

[*She looks away while he drops the bagpipes and pulls on the trousers hastily.*]

DUNCAN: Look, I do apologise, I really do, you stay here and I'll go and see what I can do about this mess.

[DUNCAN *grabs a tie, slings it round his neck and heads for the door.*]

[GABRIEL *opens it for him.*]

8. INT. CORRIDOR OUTSIDE D22. DAY 2

DUNCAN *comes slap up against* DR BEAD *and* MISS QUIM *surrounded by luggage, including a huge golfing bag.*

They are about to go into their respective cabins on either side of D22. They smile through at GABRIEL, DUNCAN *hurriedly shuts the door and carrying on fastening his tie, tries to get past.*

DR BEAD *is tall and stately, beautifully dressed, her hair in a chignon.*

MISS QUIM *is stocky and robust, tweeds and pearls, rather untidy.*

They both have post BBC calling the World voices. They stare at DUNCAN'*s dishevelment.*

DUNCAN: Ladies . . .

[*He makes a little bow and tries to get past, but* MISS QUIM *shoots out a hefty paw.*]

MISS QUIM: Good morning. Gwendoline Quim at your service. May I introduce my colleague, Doctor Angela Bead?

[DUNCAN *now has tie done up. He shakes hands with them both. He wants to get away.*]

DUNCAN: Delighted. Duncan Stewart, always at your disposal.

DR BEAD: Do forgive me Mr Stewart, but as a medical lady I feel I ought to tell you that your trousers are unbuttoned.

[DUNCAN *grabs his flies in horror and shame. Squeezes past* DR BEAD *and* MISS QUIM, *who watch him rush up the stairs.*]

9. INT. D22. DAY 2

GABRIEL *is moving Duncan's mess. She makes a pile of his things, dumps them on top of a chair, whisky bottle on top of the lot.*

She gets down her own little suitcase and starts to unpack. Hangs up her two good dresses carefully.

Gets out a photograph in a frame. The photograph is of Vesuvia and two men we don't recognise. One old and grisled, [Thomas], the other young and handsome, [Michael]. She kisses the photograph and places it carefully on the dressing table.

She takes out a battered flying jacket. Holds it up to her.

GABRIEL *gets out a large guidebook of England. Opens it and looks at the flyleaf. The inscription says 'To my only angel, so that she knows how to find me. Love Michael'.*

GABRIEL *runs her finger over the words as though she's trying to feel the texture of them. She looks emotional. It's a significant moment that we can't interpret.*

It's broken by DUNCAN *crashing back in. His tie is askew.*

GABRIEL *closes the book briskly.*

DUNCAN: Don't kill the bearer of bad news. This boat is packed to the port-holes and we'll have to make do. Like me, they assumed you were a man. Gabriel's a man's name.

[*He goes over to his pile of stuff. Stares at it mournfully.*]

GABRIEL: No it's not.

DUNCAN: What about the angel? The Angel Gabriel, he was a man.

GABRIEL: How do you know, it doesn't say so?

[GABRIEL *picks up a Bible from her suitcase. Offers it to* DUNCAN.]

[*He waves it away and picks up his whisky bottle instead.*]

DUNCAN: It's obvious. Women didn't go out on their own in those days.

GABRIEL: She had wings.

[*Pause.*]

GABRIEL: My Grand-daddy Thomas was fond of the Bible. He said it clearly directs that human beings are meant to fly.

DUNCAN: I wish he'd told me that before I booked my passage on this ship.

GABRIEL: He's dead.

[DUNCAN *looking right at her:*]

DUNCAN: Gabriel Angel ... It's a lovely name. Look, bottom bunk?

GABRIEL: Top. I like heights.

[*Before* DUNCAN *can speak, there is a terrible crashing from next door. Miss Quim's cabin.*

MISS QUIM: [*disembodied voice*] Dash it. Damn thing!

[GABRIEL *goes to the wall and knocks hard.*]

[*Shouts through.*]

GABRIEL: Is everything all right in there?

MISS QUIM: [*disembodied*] Perfectly all right. Thank you very much. Gwendoline Quim here. Who are you?

GABRIEL: Gabriel Angel. Pleased to meet you.

MISS QUIM: Slip with the number seven I fear.

[*Another series of bangs and crashes comes from next door. Then a tinkling smashing glass sound.*]

[DUNCAN *takes another swig from the bottle and looks fearfully at the wall.*]

[*At that second, there's a soft rap at the door and a* BLACK STEWARD *pops his head round to see* GABRIEL *pressed up against the wall and* DUNCAN *swigging. His eyes widen.*]

DUNCAN: Steward! Why not join the party?

[*The* STEWARD *comes in tentatively, carrying a clip-board.*]

STEWARD: I've come about the Amateur Dramatics evening, Sir.

DUNCAN: Is this a ship or a side-show?

[*Another smashing sound from Miss Quim's cabin.*]

GABRIEL: I was born in a side-show.

[DUNCAN *and the* STEWARD *stare at her: both taken aback. The* STEWARD *tries to carry on as normal.*]

STEWARD: On the last night we always stage a ship's entertainment. Perhaps you would like to play the bagpipes, Sir?

DUNCAN: No thank you Steward.

[GABRIEL *picks up her guidebook from the dressing table. Opens it and reads out loud.*]

GABRIEL: It says here – [*she thumbs quickly*] – bagpipes are the National Instrument of Scotland.

DUNCAN: Very good. But I shan't be playing them. They're far too noisy.

GABRIEL: You could practise down by the engine room.

DUNCAN: No! No! Don't ask me.

[*The poor* STEWARD *is totally left out here.*]

GABRIEL: Why not?

DUNCAN: Because I don't like to say no to a lady.

GABRIEL: Say yes then.

DUNCAN: No!

[*The* STEWARD *slips out unnoticed.*]

10. INT. CORRIDOR OUTSIDE D22. DAY 2

The STEWARD *straightens himself. The* STEWARD *knocks on* MISS QUIM'S *door.*
MISS QUIM:[*V.O.*] Yes!

11. INT. MISS QUIM'S CABIN. DAY 2

The STEWARD *enters.*

MISS QUIM *is standing up practising her golfing swing. She has smashed the dressing table mirror. She hasn't started to unpack. Her blouse is untucked from her skirt.*

This is a bad day for the STEWARD.

STEWARD: Amateur Dramatics, Miss?

MISS QUIM: Last night entertainment? For thirty years I've been in charge of the nativity play. You know, Mary, Joseph, the donkey, three wise men. The nativity play and the golf club.
[MISS QUIM *takes another swing.*]
[*The* STEWARD *ducks behind the door.*]

MISS QUIM: Leave it with me Steward. You can depend on me.

12. INT. ENGINE ROOM AND CORRIDORS. DAY 2

The thud of the engine room. The bowels of the boat.

GABRIEL *is exploring the ship. She looks into the steamy haze of the engine room.*

We see pipe wheels and vents. Everything looks overlarge and strange. Great hisses of steam erupt and break.

A GROUP OF BLACK MEN *stripped to the waist are shovelling coal into a roaring fiery furnace.*

At a small folding card table TWO WHITE MEN *sit playing poker. By their side is a Union Jack stuck in a pot of sand.*

GABRIEL *is the voyeur. Nobody notices her.*

13. INT. PASSAGE. (ENGINE ROOM). DAY 2

She passes on down a dark narrow passage, the boom boom of the ship in her ears, she sees a little ladder, climbs it onto a higher deck.

14. INT. FIRST CLASS CORRIDOR. DAY 2

Ahead of her is a door marked: 'Private First Class'. She hesitates, looks back the way she's come, then carefully pushes through it.

She's in a light airy corridor: the wide cabin doors have lattice grills, most are open, GABRIEL *tiptoes down peeping in at the first classers.*

She sees a WOMAN *shaking out a full-skirted ball gown. It's sumptuous and beautiful. A* BLACK ARM *comes into view and takes it from the* WOMAN. *Puts it on a hanger.*

In a cabin on the other side a MAN *has his* WIFE *under him on the bed. He's crouched over her, laughing.*

GABRIEL *hurries by.*

At another lattice a WOMAN *takes off her wig and puts it on a wig stand.*

GABRIEL *comes to the end door and peeps in. A distinguished* THIN MAN *in his late fifties is dressed in a safari suit, intently painting a watercolour of the dockside.*

This is REX GOODYEAR.

REX GOODYEAR *has a clean tidy palette. He paints wearing white gloves which have just a couple of red spots on them.*

Hung behind the easle is a full dress penguin suit.

GABRIEL *watches fascinated. She stands on tiptoe to see better. Suddenly she hears a noise.*

A previous door opens and a BLACK MAID *comes out. She looks at* GABRIEL *peering in.*

GABRIEL *drops away from the door and looks back at her.*

A moment of recognition, of unease, of uncertainty.

GABRIEL *turns, pushes the door ahead of her marked 'Deck'.*

15. EXT. DECK. DAY 2

GABRIEL *pushes through the door into blinding brilliant sunshine: a contrast to the subdued coolness of the first class. The sun is in her face. She shields her eyes, blinking at the sun. At the same moment as she passes out through the door, someone takes a photograph of her.*

The PHOTOGRAPHER *lowers the camera, smiles. It's* DUNCAN.

DUNCAN: MissAngel.

[*A* WHITE WAITER *comes by with a tray, of ice-creams in little dishes. As he heads through the door into first class,* DUNCAN *lifts two ices from the tray and smiles confidently.*]

WAITER: These are for the first class, Sir.

DUNCAN: That's all right, then.

[*The* WAITER *frowns, hesitates but passes on through the door.* DUNCAN *presents one to* GABRIEL.]

GABRIEL: We're not First Class.

DUNCAN: No but we ought to be.

[DUNCAN *and* GABRIEL *stroll along the deck.*]

DUNCAN: Enjoy your little foray into the bowels?

GABRIEL: I wanted to explore. I got lost.

DUNCAN: You can only get lost if you've got somewhere to go. I never have anywhere to go, ergo, I never get lost.

GABRIEL: Aren't you going somewhere now? Back to Scotland?

DUNCAN: Scotland? Oh yes, Scotland. I don't recommend it.

GABRIEL: There's a section in my guidebook called 'The rest of England'. You're in it.

DUNCAN: I'm delighted. Why are you going to England?

GABRIEL: Why did you take my photograph?

DUNCAN: Why not? It's my job, it's how I earn a living. Oh, but don't worry, I'll give you your photograph. You can show it to your children and say 'This is how your mother came to England when she was young and pretty and photographed by a tall dark stranger'.

[DUNCAN *laughs.*]

15A. EXT. ANOTHER PART OF THE DECK. [TANK]. DAY 2

DUNCAN *and* GABRIEL *walk on.*

OTHER PEOPLE *are milling about.*

DUNCAN: What will you do, in England?

GABRIEL: I have to save up to buy an aeroplane.

DUNCAN: I beg your pardon.

[GABRIEL *turns and smiles sweetly at* DUNCAN.]

GABRIEL: I'm an aviator.

16. EXT. FLASHBACK. CARIBBEAN. RUNWAY. DAY. 1948

A dirt runway on their island.
Torrential rain.
VESUVIA *and* GABRIEL *are standing either side of a makeshift plane, each forcing round a propeller.*
THOMAS *is in the cockpit wearing a battered flying jacket and goggles.*
THOMAS: Don't let me down now, I gotta get up there. Heave it for me, heave it.
[THOMAS *wipes his face.*]
[GABRIEL *and* VESUVIA *try once more.*]
VESUVIA: You madman Thomas Angel. You go up today and you're never comin' back down and that's a fact . . .
THOMAS: You take no risks, you stay on the ground all your life like a two bit sugar picker. There's money for us if I make this run, I gotta make it.
[GABRIEL *leaves her propellor for a moment and jumps up and hangs on the cockpit.*]
GABRIEL: Let me come with you. I'll bail out the water, I can take over while you eat.
[THOMAS *lifts up his goggles and grins at* GABRIEL.]
THOMAS: And what would Michael say if his angel came home with rain on her wings?
[*He gently unhooks her hands and she drops back to her floor. There is a lull in the storm.*]
[GABRIEL *and* VESUVIA *swing the propellors round again.*]
[*The plane whines into life.*]
[GABRIEL *and* VESUVIA *drop back and* THOMAS *begins to judder down the runway.*]
THOMAS: I'll be home ahead of the moon.
[*The plane gathers speed and takes off.*]
[GABRIEL *and* VESUVIA *stand holding hands, soaking wet, watching the tail of the plane split the purple sky.*]

17. EXT. DECK – MAP. DAY 2. EARLY EVENING

REX GOODYEAR *and* DR BEAD *are walking together across the deck.* MISS QUIM *is trotting behind with a couple of* CHAPS *in army uniform. Other* PASSENGERS *are floating about.* REX *attracts attention.*

DR BEAD: Yes Professor, my colleague and I are going home too although not to receive a knighthood.

REX: [*laughing modestly but pleased*] You flatter me Dr Bead. Of course Art has been my life and one is grateful for some recognition of that but truth, truth has been my passion.

DR BEAD: You should have been a missionary.

REX: [*not so pleased*] With respect Dr Bead, God lacks the originality of an early Titian.

[DR BEAD *is not pleased. They reach the top of the stairs leading to the Lounge.* REX *indicates that* DR BEAD *should go down first.*]

DR BEAD: So would you say that you are an art expert or a lie detector?

[*She goes down the stairs.* REX *follows, trying to keep up with the barb.*]

REX: Very clever Dr Bead. Perhaps there is really no difference. Every time I expose a fake I am opening the way for a little more truth. We need certainties in this life, I'm sure we can agree on that.

[*They reach the map. Closely followed by* MISS QUIM *and the* ARMY CHAPS. *A couple of people, a* MAN *and a* WOMAN *are already standing by the map.*]

[*The map charts the ship's voyage across the Atlantic. A thin red line shows the path of the ship. The ship itself is represented by a 3-D model which can be moved along the line magnetically.*]

[*Next to the map is a blackboard where the ship's coordinates and the daily temperature are chalked up.*]

[REX *puts on his glasses and examines it.*]

DR BEAD: We could be going round and round in circles for all we know.

MISS QUIM: Just like life what?

[*The* ARMY CHAPS *titter weakly.* REX *ignores her and continues his scrutiny.*]

REX: I see. [*To the assembled*] Every day one of the crew will move

15

the vessel along and change the coordinates. You see this vertical black line here?

[*He points in a schoolmasterly fashion to a thin black line cutting across the red line of the journey.* GABRIEL *comes up to the group and listens quietly. We don't see* DUNCAN *but he is behind her.*]

REX: In four days we'll be precisely mid-ocean. Nothing but sea.

DUNCAN: The point of no return.

[REX *jerks his head suddenly in Duncan's direction.* REX *looks appalled, confused. His certainty gone.*

REX: Good God. Alasdair Birch!

[*All the assembled look at* DUNCAN. DUNCAN *looks behind him. Looks back at* REX *and smiles pleasantly.*]

DUNCAN: Alasdair Birch?

REX: [*recovering himself*] I'm sorry, I thought for a second that I recognised you. It was your voice and the way your face suddenly caught the light. You remind me very much of a friend I once had in Cairo.

DUNCAN: A friend?

REX: Ha, ha, it was a long time ago and he certainly wasn't a Scot. [REX *holds out his hand.*]

REX: Rex Goodyear. Pleased to meet you.

DUNCAN: [*shaking hands*] Duncan Stewart at your service. Of course I recognise you Professor. One of England's famous faces.

[REX *smiles deprecatingly. There is a little flutter amongst the group.*]

DR BEAD: Oh Mr Stewart . . . we meet again.

[DUNCAN *checks his flies.*]

REX: [*intently but surprised*] You know one another?

MISS QUIM: Ships that pass in the night . . .

22. INT. THE BAR AND DANCE FLOOR. DAY 2. EARLY EVENING.

A FEW PEOPLE *are about.*

A BLACK PIANIST *plays smooth tunes on a white piano.*

DR BEAD *and* GABRIEL *take a table.*

MISS QUIM *collars the* BARTENDER *and hives him off conspiratorially.*

DR BEAD: So ... England, the Promised Land. I haven't been home for thirty years, Gabriel. 1927. My father had a new Bentley that year. Do you know I half expect him to meet me at Southampton just as he dropped me off? You see time and the heart don't always make sense to one another.

GABRIEL: Nor the heart and the body it beats in.

[DR BEAD *is taken aback. She scrutinises* GABRIEL.]

DR BEAD: Gwen, Miss Quim, and I are missionaries. Retired missionaries since yesterday morning after 30 years in the service of our Lord . . . of course it helps one to believe. In God. Believing in God does reconcile the heart and the body in which it beats.

[*She touches her heart with some uncertainty*.]

DR BEAD: It does beat . . . though more quietly these days.

[*This is an awkward moment. Fortunately* MISS QUIM *arrives, clutching three huge cocktails. She plonks them down in front of the others and herself.*]

MISS QUIM: Tuck in Gabriel. When I was your age, I longed to travel. Open air, adventure. Just like Dick Whittington and his cat.

DR BEAD: Gabriel, Dick Whittington was a poor boy who set off to find his fortune and became Lord Mayor of London.

MISS QUIM: Thanks to his cat. I like a good animal story.

GABRIEL: London. The streets are paved with gold.

DR BEAD: They might have been my dear, at one time, these days you'll need a metal detector.

GABRIEL: I'm going to seek my fortune.

MISS QUIM: Quite right, what else is life for?

DR BEAD: Have you got a plastic mac? England is a very rainy country.

MISS QUIM: There you go dampening the girl's spirits. When I was your age Gabriel, I could have walked round the world with nothing but a packet of sweets.

[DUNCAN *appears at the table. He's dressed for dinner in a dark evening suit and a Stewart tartan bow-tie.*]

17

DR BEAD: Punctuality is a virtue Mr Stewart but it's only half past five.

DUNCAN: Ah Dr Bead, can a man ever be too early for his wife? [*He smiles gallantly at* GABRIEL *who looks gob smacked. She starts to speak but the others pull ahead. What can she do?*]

MISS QUIM: It's the bow-tie that fascinates me.

DR BEAD: I'm sorry that we can't ask you and your wife to join us for dinner but we're promised to Professor Goodyear. Who knows? Perhaps I can bring him a little closer to our Saviour.

DUNCAN: Where is he?

DR BEAD: Our Saviour?

MISS QUIM: No! The Professor. D'you know he has devoted his entire life to seeking out and exposing forgeries of Old Masters?

DR BEAD: [*not entirely seriously*] Without him we should barely know the truth from the lie.

[DUNCAN *takes* GABRIEL's *arm. She stands up bewildered.*]

DUNCAN: If a painting's good then it's good. Does it matter who painted it? [*He whisks* GABRIEL *away from the table and into the lounge. He is confident, talkative, as if his behaviour is normal. As if they are married.*]

19. INT. LOUNGE. DAY 2. EARLY EVENING

DUNCAN: You meet so many oddballs at sea. It's much safer to stay at home. Fancy a stroll?

GABRIEL: Mr Stewart, you are not my husband.

DUNCAN: Oh dear. Don't you think I'd make a very fine husband? [DUNCAN *preens himself in the mirror in the lounge.*]

GABRIEL: Mr Stewart. You and I are not married.

DUNCAN: I admit it, we're not. But it was the two old ladies I was thinking of, how will they feel when they find out you're sharing a cabin with a man you hardly know?

GABRIEL: I don't want to share it with you.

DUNCAN: All right. Frankly Miss Angel, there are plenty of black girls prepared to get a passage to England by offering themselves to any single man who'll share a bunk.

[GABRIEL *realises what he means. She slaps him just as the*

BLACK STEWARD *walks by. The* STEWARD *stops in his tracks and backs into a corner. He doesn't want any more of* DUNCAN *and* GABRIEL *just yet. From his position he is witness to the scene and to* REX *suddenly staring at* DUNCAN's *back view in his intent way.*]

DUNCAN: Hey!

[DUNCAN *grabs* GABRIEL's *arm quite roughly.*]

GABRIEL: I'm not that kind of woman.

[*She pulls away.*]

DUNCAN: [*softly*] And I'm not that kind of man.

[DUNCAN *holds out both his hands.*]

[GABRIEL *hesitates and then turns and walks through the door marked 'Lower deck'.*]

[DUNCAN *is left standing staring after Gabriel.*]

[*From the gap in between the lounge and the bar, we see* REX GOODYEAR *staring at him.*]

20. INT. CORRIDORS. DAY 2. EARLY EVENING

GABRIEL *is walking quickly. She walks past a row of linen tubs on wheels.* TWO BLACK MAIDS *are taking out clean laundry from one of the tubs. They look at her but don't speak. She passes on. As she passes the kitchens, the green baize doors swing open.*

21. INT. CORRIDOR – KITCHEN. DAY 2. EARLY EVENING

GABRIEL *looks in and sees a* ROW OF BLACKS *chopping identical vegetables with identical knives. They chop in swift unison.*

The only sound is the sound of knives. They all look up at her suddenly. She backs away.

21A. INT. CORRIDOR OF SHOPS. DAY 2. EARLY EVENING

GABRIEL *passes a gift shop, poodle parlour and beauty salon.*

19

22. INT. CORRIDOR OUTSIDE D22/BATHROOM. DAY 2 EARLY EVENING

She comes to her own corridor, but goes into the bathroom.

A BLACK WOMAN *is on her hands and knees in front of the open toilet cubicle. She's polishing the tiles.*

GABRIEL *quickly redoes her lipstick. The* WOMAN *mops.* GABRIEL *goes into D22.*

23. INT. D22. DAY 2. EARLY EVENING

GABRIEL *kicks off her shoes and pours herself a glass of water. She drinks deeply.*

24. INT. D22. DAY 2. EVENING

It is later. GABRIEL *is lying on the top bunk, looking at the photograph of Vesuvia, Thomas and Michael.*

25. INT. DINING ROOM. DAY 2. EVENING

DUNCAN *in his regalia, drinks heavily from his large Scotch and Soda in front of him. He looks angry.*

The WHITE WAITER *comes over.*

WAITER: Excuse me, Sir. Will Miss Angel be joining you, tonight?

DUNCAN: My wife is unwell.

[*The* WAITER *gives him a queer look, but says nothing and leaves.*]

[*The* DINERS *are eating.*]

[*Only* DUNCAN *is sitting alone. He stares straight ahead and takes another drink.*]

26. EXT: DECK. DAY 3. AFTERNOON

REX GOODYEAR *is on deck. He has a small* GROUP *surrounding him.* ONE OF THE ARMY CHAPS, *the* WOMAN *who was beside the map. A* COUPLE *on their way to play tennis.* REX *is laughing. Very much the man of the moment.*

REX: Of course I shall be delighted to give a lecture. I had no idea you were all so interested in Art.

AMERICAN WOMAN: I hope you tell us about the Titian scandal Professor. Didn't that almost ruin your career? Art expert fooled by famous forger?

[REX *looks thunderous. His easy superiority slips for a second.*]

REX: That was nine years ago my dear lady. You'll forgive me if I prefer not to live in the past.

[*He moves away from the* GROUP *who stare at him. The* WOMAN *shrugs.* REX *strides through the* PEOPLE *milling about. Suddenly he sees* GABRIEL *standing with the* BLACK STEWARD. *The* STEWARD *is filling big balloons with helium from a cylinder. Other people carry them about gaily. The* STEWARD *gives her a balloon then smiles and gives her another one. She moves away.* REX *goes after her, then slows when he reaches her as if to feign coincidence.*]

REX: Mrs Stewart? Mrs Stewart?

[GABRIEL *doesn't turn round. It's not her name.*]

REX: It is Mrs Stewart?

[GABRIEL *turns now that* REX *is down her ear. She looks surprised. Then we see her decide to play the part. We see it in her face.*]

We met last night, but only briefly, because I didn't see you with the ladies after dinner. Only your husband. Professor Rex Goodyear.

[REX *holds out his hand.*]

GABRIEL: Pleased to meet you. Please call me Gabriel.

[GABRIEL *hands* REX *a balloon. Reluctantly he takes it.*]

REX: And what do I do with this?

GABRIEL: Write your name on the luggage label. It's a race to see whose balloon will travel the furthest.

[REX *hands her the pen from his jacket. He watches closely as she writes Gabriel Angel on her label.*]

REX: I prefer games with more challenge than chance. Angel. That must be your maiden name.

GABRIEL: Yes, it is. Here . . .

[*She writes his name for him.*]

GABRIEL: . . . Make a wish and let it go.

21

REX: Wishing's not my style either, I'm afraid.

GABRIEL: If someone makes a wish, someone is flying their mind. If your mind doesn't fly, what can your body do but walk the same old dirt road?

REX: Better make two wishes then. I'll give you mine.

[REX *smiles awkwardly.* GABRIEL *takes the balloon.*]

GABRIEL: Isn't there anything you want enough to wish for it?

REX: What you want has a habit of slipping away?

[Scene 26 INSERT – to be filmed on the Tank: *The ship hoots. All the* PASSENGERS *let go of their balloons. The balloons make a mass of colour against the sky. End of insert.*]

[GABRIEL *holds up two balloons, her arms outstretched. She lets them go. They go in a different direction to the others.*]

[DUNCAN *is on deck with his camera equipment. He is about to photograph two female identical* TWINS *who are identically posing in identical clothes. Suddenly he sees* REX *and* GABRIEL *together. He is not happy about this but he has to go on with the photograph. His concentraton is destroyed. He tries to compose himself. He takes their photo.*]

REX: Have you been married long?

GABRIEL: Two years, but I've known my husband all my life.

REX: Really? Mr Stewart doesn't look the kind to be a childhood sweetheart.

GABRIEL: Duncan is very kind. [*she pauses*]

[REX *laughs and looks at her closely.*]

REX: Mr Stewart reminds me so much of someone I once knew very well. Better than I knew my own wife. She was entirely unpredictable. He at least had some rules I could follow.

GABRIEL: Is your wife travelling with you, Professor?

REX: My wife is dead.

GABRIEL: I'm sorry.

REX: She was murdered.

[GABRIEL *recoils.* DUNCAN *comes hurrying over with his gear. He sees* GABRIEL *is upset.*]

DUNCAN: Professor. I had no idea you were interested in balloons.

REX: I bumped into your charming wife and we were passing the time. I believe she has made a wish on my behalf and sent it by balloon to wherever it wishes to go. She's far more optimistic about the world than I am, but then perhaps it has not yet deceived her. Do excuse me.

[*Exit* REX.]

[DUNCAN *steers* GABRIEL *towards a line of deck chairs.*]

DUNCAN: What's the matter Gabriel? What did he say to you?

[GABRIEL *doesn't want to sit down.*]

GABRIEL: Nothing. It's nothing. He told me his wife had been killed.

[GABRIEL *is clearly upset.*]

DUNCAN: I see. I see. He wasn't asking about me then?

[GABRIEL *looks at him oddly.*]

GABRIEL: Why should he? He doesn't know you?

DUNCAN: No. [*he pauses*] So you didn't tell him anything about me?

GABRIEL: I don't know anything about you.

[GABRIEL *moves swiftly away.* DUNCAN *hesitates for a moment, then goes after her but he's hampered by his equipment. A crowd of people suddenly block her from his view. He pushes through but she's gone.*]

27. INT. CORRIDOR OUTSIDE D22. DAY 3

REX *knocks at the cabin door. Tries it. Goes in.*

27A. INT. D22. DAY 3

REX *searches quickly and expertly through Duncan's things. Finds his passport. It says Duncan Stewart. Photographer.*

REX *looks for Gabriel's passport. Finds it in the dressing-table drawer. As he tries to open it, he hears a sound outside. Quickly he hides in the wardrobe, taking the passport with him.*

DUNCAN *opens the door. Looks around. Puts down his camera and goes out again.*

REX *slips out. Listens to* DUNCAN's *footsteps, then leaves the cabin quickly, shoving the passport back in the drawer rather carelessly.*

27B. INT. CORRIDOR OUTSIDE D22. DAY 3

REX *hurries up the steps.*

DUNCAN *opens the bathroom door opposite and stares after him.*

28. EXT. DECK. DAY 3

DR BEAD *and* MISS QUIM, *leaning on the rail, eating icecreams. They're talking together.*

DR BEAD: If we're going to put on a play, let's have a mediaeval morality play.

MISS QUIM: Can't we have a panto?

DR BEAD: No, Gwen, we cannot have a panto.

MISS QUIM: Well all right, have it your own way, but who's going to play the Devil?

[REX *arrives, smiling.*]

DR BEAD: Professor Goodyear. How timely. You'll come to our play rehearsal tomorrow, won't you? We're going to do Massinger's '*The Temptation*'.

REX: I can't act, I fear.

MISS QUIM: Don't worry, none of us can.

DR BEAD: Do come. We've persuaded Mr and Mrs Stewart. We all have a part to play. You can be whoever you like.

REX: If only that were true. Well, if the Stewarts are to be there, then I must be there. Can't let the side down. Ladies, excuse me while I go and practise in front of the mirror.

[*He gives a little bow and exits.*]

[DR BEAD *and* MISS QUIM *are still leaning on the rail.*]

DR BEAD: Don't you like a man with a sense of humour?

[MISS QUIM *gives a little snort.*]

[*No Scene 29*]

30. INT. PURSER'S OFFICE. DAY 3.

REX: Could I see a copy of the cabin lists, please?

[*The* PURSER *pushes one across his little window.*]

[REX *runs through the list until he finds D22. It says Mr Duncan Stewart. Mr Gabriel Angel. The names have an asterisk beside them.* REX *looks up the asterisk mark. It says 'Booking Error'.*]

31. EXT. BOAT. DAY 3. EVENING.

A shot of the ship like a bath-time boat under the stars. Serene, purposeful.

32. EXT. DECK. DAY 3. EVENING.

On deck, GUESTS *are strolling about under coloured lights.*

33. INT. DINING ROOM. DAY 3. EVENING.

In the empty dining room, a line of CHEFS, *black, white, black, white, in tall white hats, come in a line through the baize swing door.*

They carry silver tureens for the tables. A huge mirror distorts their reflection as they pass.

34. INT. DR BEAD'S CABIN. DAY 3. EVENING.

In her cabin, DR BEAD *is putting on her exquisite jewellery.*

35. INT. MISS QUIM'S BATHROOM. DAY 3. EVENING.

In the bathroom, MISS QUIM *is having a strip wash. She sings.*

36. INT. D22. DAY 3. EVENING.

DUNCAN *and* GABRIEL *are getting changed on either side of a line of Duncan's clothes.*

They can't see each other.

GABRIEL *has the mirror side.*

DUNCAN *is putting on his full kilt gear.*

DUNCAN: The Duncan Stewart Modesty Changing Rail. Patent Pending.

[DUNCAN *pops his head over the rail and blows* GABRIEL *a little kiss.*]
[GABRIEL *laughs.*]

37. INT. BAR/DANCE FLOOR. DAY 3. NIGHT

DUNCAN *and* GABRIEL *walk into the bar.*
The band plays lively dance music.
GUESTS *are dancing and drinking.*
REX GOODYEAR *sits at a little table to one side.*
DUNCAN *is heading for the bar.*

GABRIEL *touches his arm and smiles. She wants to dance. They take the floor and dance. Not intimate. Fun. They are both good but Gabriel's better.*

GABRIEL: Miss Quim's going to teach me to play golf. Everyone in England plays golf. It's an old English game.

DUNCAN: Would you care to play a game with me? An old Scottish game called Truth or Dare. You see, I can ask you anything and you have to answer and you can ask me anything and I'll answer. The one who dares to tell the most truth wins. Don't you get tired of keeping secrets?

GABRIEL: I haven't got any secrets.

DUNCAN: Never mind, you can have some of mine. When I was young, as young as you, I thought I might make money, make a name for myself, get married, have something in my hands for middle age, but all I've collected are other people's secrets and a few of my own.

GABRIEL: If you really had nothing you'd have nothing to hide.

[DUNCAN *laughs and looks at her with some admiration. Like Dr Bead, he's finding that* GABRIEL *is sharp.*]

GABRIEL: Grand-daddy Thomas had nothing. He worked for the mail company loading sacks but while he was loading he was learning. He learned how to fly. He volunteered when the weather was so bad that no white man would risk leaving the ground. They let him do it cause they had to. After that he made all the bad runs for half the price of a white man on a fine day. That plane was the most worn out beast I ever saw.

DUNCAN: [*panting*] Worse than me?

[*The music stops briefly.* DUNCAN *is panting.*]

GABRIEL: Maybe not. He never got his pilot's licence.

[DUNCAN *ushers* GABRIEL *off the floor to a table.*]

DUNCAN: Thank God I don't need a licence to dance.

GABRIEL: You wouldn't get it.

[DUNCAN *looks wounded. He signals to the* WAITER *and the two sit down.*]

DUNCAN: Do you have to do the same thing as your grandfather.

GABRIEL: Thomas used to tell us, that's Michael and me, how our ancestors worked in the fields with chains on their feet. They sang songs to one another about wings. About wings pushing from their shoulderblades, wings lifting them away from the sun without shade and the irons that tied them to the dust. When Thomas learned to fly he was trying to carry their dream.

[*The* WAITER *arrives with a scotch for* DUNCAN *and a frothy thing for* GABRIEL.]

DUNCAN: In my experience dreams are too heavy to carry alone.

[*He flips a coin out of his pocket and spins it in the air.*]

DUNCAN: Heads I start, Tails you don't.

[*He glances at the coin.*]

DUNCAN: Truth or Dare, who's Michael? Your brother?

GABRIEL: Not exactly. We were brought up together. We were both orphans. Vesuvia took us in because she said that the nuns taught a child to look down all the time and that life is the science of looking up.

DUNCAN: You're a funny sort of a girl.

GABRIEL: Michael said that where the other girls have breasts I have propellers.

DUNCAN: How would he know?

[*He doesn't like this.*]

[*At that second* MISS QUIM *swoops over. She's wearing a tux, pearls, skirt and patent leather dance shoes. She looks great in a Quim-like way.* GABRIEL *smiles up at her. She likes Miss Quim.*

MISS QUIM: Care to take a turn Gabriel?

[MISS QUIM *offers her arm.* GABRIEL *stands up.* DUNCAN *is sulking.*]

DUNCAN: How would he know?

[*The* BAND *starts playing.* MISS QUIM *turns away for a second.*

27

GABRIEL *leans down towards* DUNCAN.]

GABRIEL: Michael's my husband.

[GABRIEL *and* MISS QUIM *get onto the dance floor.* DUNCAN *stands up and heads for the bar. He's angry and wrong-footed. As he stands waiting to be served* REX GOODYEAR *comes alongside him.*]

REX: Scotch isn't it?

DUNCAN: For tonight. Thank you.

[REX *signals to the* BARMAN *who comes at once.*]

[DUNCAN *passes his hip flask over.*]

REX: They say a man can change everything except his tipple.

DUNCAN: Really? I've no preference myself. I find scotch steadies the sea-sickness.

[REX *nods and turns towards the dancefloor where* MISS QUIM *and* GABRIEL *are whirling about.*]

REX: Been married long?

DUNCAN: Five years. We're settling in Scotland.

[REX *reacts.*]

REX: Forgive me if I stare, you see your resemblance to my friend is quite uncanny. Quite remarkable.

[*The* WAITER *puts down two glasses and the hip flask on the bar.* DUNCAN *pockets the flask and drinks from his glass.*]

DUNCAN: There are very few faces in the world, Professor. We like to think of ourselves as individuals. Look closer and we're all one of a kind.

REX: Ah, now you even sound like him.

DUNCAN: Who?

REX: Alasdair Birch. He was a friend of my wife. He was the last person to see her alive.

[REX *looks troubled. For a moment, his arrogance and disdain give way to vulnerability and confusion.*]

DUNCAN: And you haven't seen him since?

REX: I see his name on every hotel register. I see his face in every crowd. Sometimes I think I see his face in my own mirror. [*pause*] But no, I haven't seen him since.

DUNCAN: Have you tried looking him up in the telephone directory?

[REX *is enraged at this cheap cut. His face tightens.*]

[*Before he can speak* DR BEAD *comes over to them. She is wearing a Fortuny dress. She looks wonderful. The* MEN *virtually stand to attention. They have to be polite now.* DR BEAD *has that kind of authority and presence.*]

REX: Dr Bead. A glass of champagne?

DR BEAD: Thank you but I am absolutely tee-total.

[*She gazes at Duncan's large scotch. He puts it down.*]

DUNCAN: Sea-sickness tonic.

DR BEAD: I'm looking for Gwen . . .

[*As she says this she turns to the dance floor where* MISS QUIM *and* GABRIEL *are fox-trotting like crazy.* GABRIEL *is laughing.* MISS QUIM *is puffing like an engine, but she's very good. The music comes to an end and the pair roll towards the bar.*]

DR BEAD: Gwen, you will certainly have a heart-attack and die without enjoying your retirement.

MISS QUIM: This *is* my retirement and I *am* enjoying it.

DR BEAD: Gabriel, gentlemen, pleasant dreams for all. Come along Gwen, doctor's orders.

[*They depart arm in arm,* MISS QUIM *chattering and protesting as the three watch them leave the room.*]

DUNCAN: One with a face like a cricket ball. The other like a love-note somebody crushed up in their fist.

REX: Lesbians.

GABRIEL: Is that a kind of missionary?

REX: So I'm told. I'm sure your husband will explain.

[*Exit* REX. *The lights are low.* PEOPLE *are drifting away.*]

DUNCAN: A last dance, Miss Angel?

[*They move onto the floor. It's a slow number. They are getting closer.*]

DUNCAN: Truth or Dare, does your husband dance?

GABRIEL: When he can.

DUNCAN: Does he put his hand on your back like this?

GABRIEL: Tell me about Scotland.

DUNCAN: Read your guidebook, I'm not much use.

GABRIEL: Can't you remember what it's like?

DUNCAN: Dancing like this, with a woman? No.

GABRIEL: Scotland.

DUNCAN: I'm not a Scot.

[GABRIEL *pulls back. She doesn't know what to make of this.*]

38. EXT. DAY 3. NIGHT

A shot of the moon.

39. INT. MISS QUIM'S CABIN. DAY 3. NIGHT

MISS QUIM *sitting in her even more wrecked cabin. She's typing furiously on a dinky portable.*

40. INT. DR BEAD'S CABIN. DAY 3. NIGHT

DR BEAD, *her hair down, asleep.*

41. INT. REX GOODYEAR'S CABIN. DAY 3. NIGHT

REX GOODYEAR *is sitting on his bed surrounded by newspaper articles with various headings about 'famous forger'. Also on the bed is a photograph of a very beautiful woman and a man who could be Duncan, perhaps ten years ago.*

42. INT. D22. DAY 3. NIGHT

DUNCAN *and* GABRIEL *are in their separate bunks. Both lie with their eyes open, staring up.*
DUNCAN: Are you asleep?
GABRIEL: Yes.
DUNCAN: So am I.
 [DUNCAN *pauses.*]
GABRIEL: Why are you pretending to be Scottish?
DUNCAN: Doesn't everyone pretend about themselves from time to time? Especially in public.
GABRIEL: They don't pretend to be Scottish.
DUNCAN: Let's say I loved somebody who loved me. She's dead now and since that day I haven't known who I am. So for the time being, I might as well be a Scotsman.
GABRIEL: How did she die?

DUNCAN: She drowned. [*he sighs*] She had to have her own way, and in the end it killed her.

GABRIEL: Living someone else's way kills you too.

DUNCAN: She thought she was stronger than the waves, but she was wrong. The waves are stronger.

[GABRIEL *leans down and looks at* DUNCAN.]

GABRIEL: I'm sorry.

DUNCAN: It was a long time ago. Truth or Dare. What about Michael? Isn't he very much alive.

GABRIEL: Very much. We've always been together. He's in England now. I'm going to be with him. He's made money, done well. That's him in the photograph.

[DUNCAN *looks across at the photograph, dim under the dim light.*]

GABRIEL: He always told me that England is the Promised Land.

DUNCAN: Does he fly like you?

GABRIEL: No, he holds the string. I need that.

DUNCAN: Do you?

42A. INT. D22. DAY 3. LATER. NIGHT.

GABRIEL *is lying awake.* DUNCAN *is sound asleep and snoring slightly.* GABRIEL *leans over and looks at him. Lies back deep in thought.*

43. INT. BALLROOM. DAY 4. AFTERNOON.

DR BEAD *and* MISS QUIM *have dropped a red velvet curtain at the back of the stage where the Band play.*

Two large boxes marked props are at either side of the stage. A large puppet figure hangs out of one of them, swaying a little. There are two bolts of opulent cloth on the stage and a large shape under a dust-sheet.

In the background, DUNCAN *and* REX *are struggling with a cardboard cut-out of Satan. Full size, with a cloak and horns and a red tongue. They try and make it stand up.*

In the foreground, DR BEAD *and* MISS QUIM *are sitting with a script each.*

DR BEAD: I thought we were doing The Temptation.

MISS QUIM: That's right, Angela. Thing is, it's *my* Temptation, I wrote it myself last night.

[GABRIEL *rushes in.*]

MISS QUIM: Perfect!

[*She rummages under the sheet and struggles to lift up something bulky that we can't yet see.*

She sets about fastening whatever it is onto GABRIEL.]

MISS QUIM: You'll be the angel, my dear.

DR BEAD: Very good, but who's going to play the Devil?

DUNCAN: Surely it will have to be our Professor. Wasn't the Devil an Englishman?

REX: [*coldly*] I thought that was God.

DUNCAN: All the better then to cast against type.

REX: You have the face for the part.

MISS QUIM: [*firmly*] Mr Stewart will play the Devil, Professor Goodyear will play the character of Morality. Morality spots everyone else's sins in the play, but never his own. Angela, you be the Narrator and I will play The Fool.

[MISS QUIM *dishes out the scripts, picks up her mallet and bangs the piano.* GABRIEL *turns to the* OTHERS *and suddenly in full view reveals that she is wearing a pair of great golden wings.* GABRIEL *begins as if with her script lines, but moves into the flashback.*]

44. EXT. FLASHBACK. CARIBBEAN HUT. DAY. 1940

GABRIEL: It was in the year 1703 in the country of Portugal. Father Bartolomeu came up with the idea of flying. He liked to imagine the angels with their great gold wings cut across the sun and their bodies bright as dragonflies.

[GABRIEL *is a little girl, about eight. She's naked except for a pair of gold wings strapped to her. She seems to be flying across the front of Vesuvia's shack. Back and forth she flies.*]

[*We hear laughter.* THOMAS *comes into shot. He's operating a pulley that swings the* LITTLE CHILD.]

[VESUVIA *is sitting playing a small guitar.* MICHAEL *sits at her feet reading a comic book. He doesn't look up.*]

THOMAS: Don't want to be like Icarus, little girl. Icarus flew too near the sun and the sun took revenge on his wings and melted the wax that bound the feathers until the feathers fell away and Icarus fell.

[*He unhooks* LITTLE GABRIEL *and cuddles her.*]

THOMAS: The trick is to get some place in between. The earth will pull you down and the sun will burn you up. Gotta be smarter than the earth and the sun.

[THOMAS *lifts her out at arm's length. She laughs.*]

THOMAS: But I say you will Gabriel Angel. I know you will.

[*End flashback.*]

45. EXT. DECK. DAY 4. EARLY EVENING

MISS QUIM *is putting into an automatic putter.* DR BEAD *is standing by reading the play.*

DR BEAD: He opens her dress and traces the outline of her breast. He says, 'Your breasts are beehives pouring honey.' It's a little on the steamy side, Gwen.

MISS QUIM: Got to be, Angela. It's called The Temptation.

DR BEAD: I didn't know you were so intimate with the compulsions of the flesh.

MISS QUIM: Ha, well. Don't you ever feel that we might have missed out on a few slices of life in the past thirty years?

[*She thwacks her ball over the heads of a nuclear family and into the sea.*]

DR BEAD: Don't torment yourself with questions like that. Everyone makes their choices, we made ours.

MISS QUIM: You know Angela, what I really wanted was to work for Thomas Cook.

[DR BEAD *looks aghast. Opens her mouth. Shuts it again.*]

MISS QUIM: As a tour leader. I wanted to travel. They didn't take girls though.

[*She pats her portly frame.*]

MISS QUIM: Yes, I was a girl once. So I thought, 'Right Oh, I'll be a missionary. They get a bit of travelling in.'

DR BEAD: So it wasn't the Saviour then?

MISS QUIM: 'Fraid not, old girl. Are you frightfully upset?

DR BEAD: A little surprised. I thought I knew you.

46. INT. CABIN D22. DAY 4. EVENING

GABRIEL *is alone in the cabin. She's wearing her best dress. She looks beautiful. She puts a few finishing touches to herself, dwells on her eyes, her lips, her neck. She's enjoying herself. She opens the dressing-table drawer for a bottle of cologne. Her hand strays instead to a bundle of letters wrapped in a ribbon. She takes them out, unwraps them, they are all folded at the signature, 'Love Michael.' The last one isn't opened. She hesitates at the envelope, then she quickly re-wraps the bundle, opens the built-in wardrobe and reaches up to the top shelf.*

As GABRIEL *puts down the letters, she feels something, on the top shelf. She pulls it down with difficulty, it's a roll of canvas. She brings it into the cabin and starts to unroll it.*

47. INT. DINING ROOM. DAY 4. EVENING

REX *is dining alone.*

DR BEAD *and* MISS QUIM *are together with another* COUPLE *we don't know. They are talking enthusiastically, much animation.*

Other DINERS *are arriving and settling. Hubbub.*

DUNCAN *in a dark lounge suit is sitting alone at his table, a whisky in front of him.*

The WHITE WAITER *comes over with a salver, lifts the lid, there are three live lobsters underneath, claws tightly bound.*

DUNCAN *looks at them critically, then points to one. The* WAITER *nods and goes away.*

GABRIEL *comes in looking lovely in her dress.*

REX *looks up.*

DUNCAN *stands up and kisses her gently on the cheek. He waits until she has seated herself before sitting down.*

DUNCAN: How lovely women are.

GABRIEL: Can't it be just me?

DUNCAN: It is just you. You look like all the women I've ever admired and you look like yourself.

[*He raises his glass and drinks.*]

DUNCAN: I've ordered champagne.

[*Another* WAITER *arrives with a bottle and pours.*]

[DUNCAN *drinks.* GABRIEL *drinks a little and sneezes.* DUNCAN *laughs.*]

DUNCAN: I'd like to say here's to us but somebody has beaten me to it. I'll drink a toast to Michael's good fortune shall I?

GABRIEL: Why are you always playing games?

DUNCAN: I'm a light-hearted man.

[*He reaches for* GABRIEL'*s hand.* GABRIEL *withholds it.*]

GABRIEL: What *is* your name?

DUNCAN: Whatever it is, it's not my married name.

[GABRIEL *looks stung, then upset.*]

DUNCAN: Who's the one who's got to be careful? You or me? No-one's meeting me at Southampton with an armful of flowers and a place to live. You'll have a good time here, I am a good time, and then it'll be bye bye Duncan.

GABRIEL: Stop it.

[REX GOODYEAR *appears at the table.*]

REX: Forgive me, I know this is your wedding anniversary, Mr Stewart did tell me only this afternoon when we were talking. I hate to interrupt but Mr Stewart I think you dropped this earlier and I am very anxious to return it to you.

[REX *goes off.*]

[*The white* WAITER *who has been hovering behind, arrives with the soup and puts it down.*]

[*Between them, like a sore, is a black and white photograph of a stunningly beautiful white woman.* DUNCAN *and* GABRIEL *look at it.*]

[DUNCAN *is pale and upset. He gets up, takes it over to* REX *says something briefly then returns to* GABRIEL *and drains his glass.*]

DUNCAN: Silly man. He found it on the floor where we'd been sitting. Nothing to do with me.

GABRIEL: Why did you tell him it was our anniversary.

DUNCAN: Why? Why not? He thinks we're married. Married people have anniversaries you know. But of course you know.

GABRIEL: Why did you let him go on thinking we're married?

DUNCAN: Why did you?

[GABRIEL *says nothing. She looks down.*]

35

DUNCAN: I did it to protect you. Because I care about you.

GABRIEL: Not to protect yourself? Not because you need a cover or an alibi? Was that woman your wife?

[DUNCAN *says nothing, he looks angry.*]

[REX *is watching.*]

GABRIEL: I'm useful to you aren't I? A safe cheap alibi.

[DUNCAN *pours from the champagne bottle and regards it.*]

DUNCAN: Trust me.

GABRIEL: [*her voice raised*] What kind of a fool do you think I am?

DUNCAN: A noisy one. Will you please stop it?

GABRIEL: You don't want to draw attention to your happy marriage?

DUNCAN: You're behaving badly.

GABRIEL: And you're not? It's all right to behave badly with a quiet voice and a smile on your face, but when I open my mouth because I'm angry you treat me like a child.

[DUNCAN *ignores her and eats his soup sedately. She drums her fingers on the table.*]

GABRIEL: Duncan . . .

[DUNCAN *ignores her. Goes on eating.*]

[GABRIEL *catches* REX's *eyes. He smiles coldly. She's very agitated.*]

GABRIEL: Duncan . . .

DUNCAN: If you don't mind I'd like to eat my soup in peace.

GABRIEL: Go ahead.

[*She stands up and chucks her soup over him. The dining room falls silent.*]

[*The piano stops playing.* GABRIEL *walks resolutely to the door, doesn't look back. All we can hear is the click of her low heels, then BAM! as she slams the door.*]

48. EXT. BOAT DECK. DAY 4. NIGHT

[*Towards end of scene, deck should start rolling.*]

   GABRIEL *is sitting up on one of the lifeboats. She looks out to sea.*

   DUNCAN *appears stripped to the waist holding the dinners. He stands up close to the lifeboat.*

DUNCAN: Don't be silly Gabriel.

GABRIEL: I'm not the one whose stripped to the waist holding two dinners.

[DUNCAN *laughs. Passes a plate and cutlery up to her. Leans on the rail and starts to eat his own.*]

DUNCAN: I'm not the one with two husbands.

GABRIEL: [*furious*] I haven't got two husbands.

DUNCAN: [*nodding*] True. Sad but true.

[*He swallows the last of his dinner and chucks the plate over the side.*]

[GABRIEL *is trying to calm down.*]

GABRIEL: Who are you?

DUNCAN: Duncan Stewart from Aberdeen. [*he salutes her*] I've got a birth certificate to prove it. [*he pauses*] True, it's not my birth certificate, but then one baby looks much like another. [*pause*] Won't you come down?

GABRIEL: This journey is my one chance at life.

DUNCAN: It's my last chance at life . . . Gabriel . . . come down.

[DUNCAN *holds out his arms to* GABRIEL.]

DUNCAN: We're in the same boat.

[*She smiles in spite of herself. He smiles. It's looking good again, just, when* REX GOODYEAR *appears in his penguin suit. He's smoking a small cigar.*]

REX: The night. The stars. The old moonlight of romance.

DUNCAN: Can I be of any assistance to you Professor?

REX: On the contrary, I thought I might be of some assistance to you. You dropped this earlier.

[*He produces the photograph again and offers it to* DUNCAN. GABRIEL *looks down from her lifeboat.*]

DUNCAN: Professor, did you not hear me the first time? That photograph does not belong to me.

[REX *puts the photograph back in his pocket.*]

REX: Dear me. [*he taps his head*] I quite forgot. How could I? I hope I haven't offended you? You seem offended.

DUNCAN: On the contrary, I'm very calm. The night, the stars . . .

REX: Indeed? I'm not an emotional man myself but I recognise the quality in others and usually I find it rather dangerous.

DUNCAN: We're not on stage now professor.

REX: No this is real life. Life with a past as well as a future. No doubt we are all sailing towards something but what have each of us left behind? [*he pauses*] You know you have an extraordinary look of someone I . . .

DUNCAN: Once knew in Cairo. Tell me Professor, was that before or after you authenticated a late Titian that turned out to have been painted in 1945? Still, what's four hundred years between friends?

[REX *steps forward and punches* DUNCAN *square in the jaw.* DUNCAN *falls back against the lifeboat dislodging* GABRIEL, *who falls on top of him.* REX GOODYEAR *swings her away bodily with surprising strength. He goes for* DUNCAN *again as* DUNCAN *staggers to his feet.*]

DUNCAN: I'm sorry. Did I say something to upset you?

[*He ducks under* REX'*s next swing and hits* REX *hard in the stomach in return.* REX *keels but stays on his feet.* DUNCAN *hits him again in the side of the head.* REX *passes out.*]

GABRIEL: What have you done to him?

[GABRIEL *kneels by* REX, *puts her cardigan under his head.*]

[*It's a strange moment broken by* DR BEAD *and* MISS QUIM *billowing over.*]

DR BEAD: Let me through I'm a doctor.

[*A few strays from the ship are coming up behind.*]

[DR BEAD *kneels down and takes* REX'*s pulse. She loosens his clothes.*]

DUNCAN: He insulted my wife.

DR BEAD: Professor Goodyear?

DUNCAN: Not all knights wear shining armour.

[DR BEAD, MISS QUIM *and* GABRIEL *stare at* DUNCAN. *What's he talking about?*]

[*The* BLACK STEWARD *and another* STEWARD *arrive with a stretcher and put* REX *onto it.*]

[GABRIEL *walks away from them, parting the small* CROWD *that has gathered.*]

[DUNCAN *comes to life and follows her off deck.*]

DR BEAD: I may have led a sheltered life but I know when a storm's brewing.

[*Bang! Crash! Great gales shake the ship. Heavy rain. Thunder*

*and Lightning. A tropical storm. Sudden and dramatic. Every-
one runs for cover.*]
[REX *is carried away by the* TWO STEWARDS *and* MISS QUIM.]
[*We see the deck deserted in the storm.*]

49. INT. CABIN D22. [SHIP ROLLING]. DAY 4 NIGHT.

DUNCAN *appears to be sleeping.*
  GABRIEL *climbs down from her bunk and goes to the bathroom.*

50. INT. CORRIDORS. [SHIP ROLLING]. DAY 4 NIGHT.

The door is locked. GABRIEL *sets off to find another one. As she
disappears down the corridor,* DUNCAN *gets up and follows her.*
  GABRIEL *walks carefully though the rolling corridors. The lights
are on but then the ship gives a terrific lurch and all the lights go
out except for the dim safety lights.*
  GABRIEL *feels her way along the walls. Suddenly a torch is shone
into her face. She gives a little cry.*
REX: Gabriel! Don't be afraid.
  [*We don't see his face. All* GABRIEL *can see is the torch beam on
  her own face. She moves aside.*]
GABRIEL: Professor Goodyear, you frightened me. Are you ill? Do
  you want Doctor Bead's cabin?
  [*She half turns to lead him the way. He takes her arm.*]
GABRIEL: What do you want?
REX: Want? I only want what I know I can get. Won't you come
  this way?
  [*She follows him down the corridor. Only the safety lights
  are on. The corridor gets narrower.*]

51. INT. ENGINE ROOM. [SHIP ROLLING] NIGHT 4

We can hear the boom boom of the engines.
  GABRIEL *passes the room where she saw the* BLACK MEN
earlier. The Pipe and Vent room.

The WHITE MEN, *still bare to the waist lie sleeping in hammocks strung up roughly between the pipes.*
The white MEN *are still playing cards.*

52. INT. TRUNK ROOM. [SHIP ROLLING]. NIGHT 4

REX *turns abruptly and opens a gate made of steel bars. It looks like a prison.*

GABRIEL *pulls back.*

REX *motions her inside.*

REX: Please . . .

[*In the room* REX *adjusts the beam on his torch from beam to spread. It makes a crude lantern.*]

[GABRIEL *gasps. They're in the trunk room. It's been ransacked.*]

REX: Don't be afraid. I have something to show you.

[*He unrolls a long canvas, secures it at the edges. We can't see it. Rex looks at it greedily.*]

GABRIEL: What are you doing with this painting?

REX: [*intently*] Why? Have you seen it before?

GABRIEL: No, no never. I don't understand.

[*She looks around the wrecked room.*]

[REX *laughs and gazes at the canvas.*]

REX: If a man is determined to know the truth, he will find it out at any cost. Truth has brought us to this room.

GABRIEL: I was on my way to the bathroom.

REX: Poor Gabriel. You're shivering. Let me be quick.

[*He moves towards her, takes her by the shoulders, gently but with terrible menace.*]

REX: Does Mr Stewart have a painting like this one? Exactly like this one?

GABRIEL: Why do you want two?

REX: I don't want two. I want my own. You see, my friend Alasdair Birch was a famous forger. A very talented man. A very charming man. That is with the ladies. This is one of his paintings, you might almost think it a Titian, if you knew anything about Titian's. Let's say that through an oversight on my part, the forger has the real thing and I have the forgery. All I want to do is to return to him his property and to reclaim my own. Unfortunately I cannot find it.

[*Gloomily* REX *snaps shut the roll with some savagery. A sense of great and suppressed anger.*]

GABRIEL: I can't help you.

[*She starts to back towards the door.* REX *looks up from where he's squatting with the painting.*]

REX: Truth Gabriel. Isn't that worth a little sacrifice?

[*He stands up. Gabriel listens.*]

REX: The foundation of my life has been to know what is genuine and what is not. No matter how much you wish it a fake can never be the real thing. The world is littered with fakes and fake-makers. Alasdair Birch, this painting. Don't you want a little certainly? Something solid under your feet?

[*The boat rocks violently.* GABRIEL *is thrown against* REX. *He steadies her, holds her against him. We see their faces.*]

REX: I want my painting because until I get it Alasdair Birch has my truth and I am carrying his lie.

[GABRIEL *pulls away. Looks* REX *in the face. She's calm now.*]

GABRIEL: What evidence do you have that Duncan is this man?

REX: None at all.

[GABRIEL *nods as if satisfied. She turns and leaves.* REX *is alone. He says out loud as he holds the painting.*]

REX: [*to himself*] None at all. Only nine years of searching.

53. INT. ENGINE ROOM. [SHIP ROLLING]. NIGHT 4

GABRIEL *begins her dark narrow walk back to the cabin.*
The ship is heaving badly.

GABRIEL *stretches out her arms to steady herself. As she walks past the engine room again, the head of a* SLEEPING MAN *rolls out at her. She cries out.*

The MAN *opens his eyes, looks at her upside down.* [*His hammock is stretched across the doorframe*].

GABRIEL *hurries on. In front of her is a door that says 'Danger' in big red letters. She turns a bend before she reaches it.*

54. INT. CORRIDORS. [SHIP ROLLING]. NIGHT 4

She's trying to get back as fast as she can. She trips and falls. Picks herself up, turns another corner, sees herself in a large mirror that says 'Sea Days Are Happy Days'.

Finally GABRIEL *is near the cabin.*

GABRIEL *notices the door is ajar. She approaches more slowly, pushes it open gingerly and goes inside.*

55. INT. CABIN D22. [SHIP ROLLING]. NIGHT 4

It's dark.

Suddenly a hand grabs GABRIEL *round the neck and there's a gun barrel at her head.*

GABRIEL *bites the hand.*

DUNCAN *curses and lets her go.*

DUNCAN: It's you!

GABRIEL: Who do I have to be to get a gun in my head?

DUNCAN: Sorry. It's not loaded.

[DUNCAN *strikes a match and lights the calor lamp on the wall. He closes the cabin door. Locks it.*]

[GABRIEL *is shivering.*]

[DUNCAN *gets her old flying jacket and wraps it around her. She recoils slightly at his touch.*]

DUNCAN: I thought you were Rex Goodyear.

GABRIEL: Rex? Just because you hit him you think you have to hide behind the door with a gun?

DUNCAN: I told you, he's a dangerous man. Where were you going?

GABRIEL: You didn't tell me, you haven't told me anything. But I can tell you I was going to the bathroom.

DUNCAN: You went the long way round then.

GABRIEL: I found a painting in the wardrobe. What is it?

DUNCAN: Now who's the snoop? Answer me truth or dare?

GABRIEL: It's our wardrobe. We share this cabin remember?

DUNCAN: It's something I did years ago. A hobby. It's nothing. It's nothing to do with you and me and you and me is the important thing.

GABRIEL: What's the painting?

DUNCAN: When I was a little boy there was a reproduction over my bed called St Nicholas calming the Tempest. It used to comfort me when it stormed outside.
[*Outside the storm.*]

DUNCAN: A small boat on a blue-black sea, the wind roars and the disciples huddle together in fear. Beneath the boat is a great fish, and up above, in full dress and mitre comes St Nicholas flying through the sky. The stars hang about him.

GABRIEL: What's that got to do with your painting?

DUNCAN: You're not the only one with dreams. I loved it so much I learned to copy it. Imitation is the sincerest form of flattery and I am sincere Gabriel. I have a motto in life that you might understand 'Do it from the heart or not at all.'

GABRIEL: Are you Alasdair Birch?

DUNCAN: No.

GABRIEL: Are you the man Professor Goodyear thinks you are?
[DUNCAN *shrugs and smiles.*]
[GABRIEL *starts packing a few things into her little bag.*]

DUNCAN: What are you doing?

GABRIEL: Getting out.

DUNCAN: I'll go.
[*He reaches for his jacket and tie and leaves.*]
[GABRIEL *stares at the closed door. Then she goes into the wardrobe and feels for the painting. It's gone.*]

56. EXT. FLASHBACK. SEA. FANTASY. NIGHT. 1955

GABRIEL *goes to the porthole and looks out.*

The porthole frames her face and acts as a distorting mirror as she looks into the sea set against the blue-black sky.

The stars loom, the waves are misshapen. What she sees next is shot as if through a distorting mirror. The figures are strange, theatrical, off-centre.

A small boat comes floating into view but going in the opposite direction to the liner. The boat passes slowly.

The boat is strewn with flowers. It's a bridal boat.

THOMAS *stands at the helm looking in at her.*

VESUVIA *sits in the stern, playing her guitar. Both are dressed up.*

In the centre, standing together, arm in arm, are MICHAEL *and* GABRIEL.

GABRIEL *is dressed in flowers, she wears a wreath of flowers on her head.* MICHAEL *is in a full morning suit. They are smiling, happy. They look confidently towards the porthole.*

The boat floats on, disappears.

57. EXT. BOAT DECK. DAY 5. EARLY MORNING

The deck floor is puddled and strewn with flowers. Deck chairs are blown over in skewed heaps. There's a tray on the floor full of glasses full of water. A small fish swims in one of the glasses.

The sky is dull and threatening.

The cover of Gabriel's lifeboat lifts and DUNCAN *climbs wearily out.*

DUNCAN *is wearing his last night clothes. He's unshaven and dishevelled. Tie in hand he walks glumly across the deck surveying the scene.*

58. EXT. DECK – MAP. DAY 5

DUNCAN *arrives at the map.*

The BLACK STEWARD *is alone there, changing the coordinates and moving the model ship along the red line of the map.*

The ship is now just past the vertical black line.

DUNCAN *stands behind him watching.*

DUNCAN: The point of no return.

STEWARD: [*without looking round*] Good morning Sir.

DUNCAN: [*fixing his tie*] Anything could happen I suppose. In the middle of the sea by ourselves like this. Only ourselves to answer to. Do you ever find anything happens? Anything unexpected?

STEWARD: Not as a rule Sir. The occasional disease.

DUNCAN: Alone on a wide wide sea.

[REX *comes up behind* DUNCAN *looking immaculate. Stark contrast between the men's dress.*]

[REX *is wearing an eye patch.*]

REX: Not quite.

[DUNCAN *turns quickly. Looks afraid for a moment.*]

REX: Do you shoot?

[*He indicates the way.* DUNCAN *goes ahead. The* STEWARD *watches.*]

59. INT. THE SHOOTING GALLERY. DAY 5

A volley of shots.

REX *and* DUNCAN *are firing at a target range. Their score notches up automatically.*

REX *is slightly ahead.*

REX: I hear you like taking photographs Mr Stewart. They say the camera never lies. Can the same be said of the photographer?

DUNCAN: I apologise for taunting you last night Professor but I will tell you again, that photograph is not mine.

REX: No, it's mine. It's a photograph of my wife before she was murdered. You see Mr Stewart women are not fired in a very hot kiln. They soon show their age, they crack under pressure. I thought my wife was different. I thought I could always tell the genuine article. She fell in love with Alasdair Birch. That was the first time he cheated me.

DUNCAN: And the second?

[REX *looks at him sharply and mows down his target of dancing girls.*]

REX: Doesn't everyone know that story? Titian expert fooled by famous forger? You weren't the first to throw it in my face.

DUNCAN: Wasn't I? I'm sorry.

[*What does he mean by this?* REX *wonders too.*]

REX: But that's not the whole story. Yes I was fooled and made a fool of. In the same week I lost my reputation, I was forced to resign my job and my wife ran off with the man responsible for all this.

DUNCAN: An adulterer, a thief and a fraud.

REX: I did not say he was a thief, but yes, he was. A little later I had a letter from him telling me that the painting in my possession certainly was a forgery but that he Birch had the genuine article.

It seems that my wife had helped him to exchange the two. How could I tell anyone? I was left with a secret, a lie. For nine years I have been searching for the truth.

[DUNCAN *shoots down all his targets.*]

DUNCAN: I envy you Professor. I've been searching for it all my life.

[DUNCAN *lays down his gun and looks at the automatic score. He's won.*]

60. INT. MISS QUIM'S CABIN. DAY 5

GABRIEL *is sitting in her nightdress and flying jacket.*

MISS QUIM *is in a huge paisley dressing gown, battered but expensive. She's making tea on a Primus stove.*

The cabin is a wreck. A golf club is embedded axe-like in the wall.

MISS QUIM: So your husband's not your husband and he might not be Mr Stewart. And you think he knows Rex Goodyear and you met Rex Goodyear in the middle of the night and he showed you a painting. There's a woman who's dead and there's a woman in a photograph who might be the same woman, and you feel fonder of Mr Stewart than you ought. Am I following?

[GABRIEL *nods her head gloomily.*]

[MISS QUIM *gives her a large cup of tea and offers the biscuit tin.*]

MISS QUIM: Royal Scot?

GABRIEL: I had a destination and a place to go. I'm not a fool Miss Quim, although Professor Goodyear and maybe Duncan even, think me so. I'm not a fool. I know England's not the Promised Land but neither is the Caribbean. Either you fight for your life or you lose it. But now, because of Duncan, I don't know what my life is.

MISS QUIM: My dear, why do you care so much for this man you hardly know?

GABRIEL: Now I will sound like a fool. It started with his accent, I wanted to listen to his voice all day, even when he said silly things. And then it's his eyes, he looks at me so seriously even when he's not being serious. That's part of the trouble I can't tell when he's joking and when he's not. He changes all the time, and I've been brought up to believe that a good man is a stable man. A good man is someone you can depend on. Duncan's full of sharp edges and I know that he can cut me but at least there's no blunt places in him. If Duncan is a bad man, what does it say about all the good men who looked at me without seeing me, who said my name and I never wanted to hear their voices again?

61. EXT. FLASHBACK. AEROPLANE IN FLIGHT. DAY. 1948

GABRIEL *and* THOMAS *are in the battered plane.*
  GABRIEL *is at the controls flying through a marble sky.*
  THOMAS *is eating rice and peas and cold fish.*
THOMAS: The trick is to know who you are so that you can know what you want. Most people only see what's in their eye-range Gabriel. Maybe they see it bigger or fancier, but it's still what they're used to. That's what keeps 'em two bit. The Wright brothers, Orville and Wilbur, they made bicycles but they saw aeroplanes. That's unusual. Yeah it was bitterly cold on the morning of the Seventeenth of December 1903 but they took their flyer from its shed and at half past ten, Orville, lying on the bottom wing, gave the signal for release. Wilbur ran alongside, steadying the machine as it moved down its long trolley towards infinity. Can you see the plane rising up like an angel? Immortality for twelve seconds. And how many years of faith and work for everyone of those twelve seconds?

62. EXT. DECK. OBSERVATION POLE. DAY 5

GABRIEL *climbing up and up the Observation Pole. It's a long way. She doesn't care. She's climbing out of her life. She gets to the crows nest and looks out to sea.*
  At the foot of the pole a small CROWD *have gathered anxiously.*
DR BEAD: You don't imagine she'll jump do you Gwen?
MISS QUIM: Would you?
DR BEAD: The heart and the body it beats in . . .
  [DUNCAN *pushes over before* DR BEAD *can say anymore.*]

DUNCAN: What's going on? Am I missing something?

[DR BEAD *points upward.* DUNCAN *follows her arm.*]

DUNCAN: Oh Lord. What's she doing?

DR BEAD: I was hoping you might know that.

DUNCAN: She's not going to jump is she? She'll drown.

[*He cups his hands around his mouth and shouts.*]

DUNCAN: Gabriel! Gabriel!

DR BEAD and MISS QUIM: Gabriel! *Gabriel!*

[*High above,* GABRIEL *hears her name floating up distorted by the air currents and the effect of the water. She shouts into the clouds.*]

GABRIEL: Gabriel!

[DUNCAN *is below and more and more agitated. He grabs the* BLACK STEWARD.]

DUNCAN: What are you going to do about her?

STEWARD: The Observation Pole is out of bounds to passengers Sir.

[DUNCAN *flings off his jacket and starts to climb the pole.* GABRIEL *doesn't look down. She shouts again, exhilarated.*]

GABRIEL: Gabriel! Gabriel!

DUNCAN: Gabriel!

[*The sun breaks through the clouds and covers her in light.*]

[DUNCAN *has to screw his eyes to climb. He falls into the crow's nest panting and sweating.*]

GABRIEL: Hello.

DUNCAN: Is that all you've got to say? What are you doing? You're crazy . . . Gabriel . . .

GABRIEL: On the wild nights who can call you home? Only the one who knows your name.

DUNCAN: I thought I was the one with an identity problem.

[*She kneels next to him and kisses him.*]

GABRIEL: I had to clear my head.

DUNCAN: Couldn't you have taken an aspirin?

[GABRIEL *looks down and sees the little* CROWD.]

DUNCAN: You terrified us all. I thought you were going to jump.

[GABRIEL *smiles at him as though he's a little boy saying a very silly thing. She strokes his face just once with her finger. It's*

48

tender. She's in control. He stands up and leans cautiously on the rail, tries to rearrange himself.]

DUNCAN: Gabriel I never expected to trust another person again. I'd done with trusting and then you got on this boat. You make me want to live. I thought I was a man with nothing but secrets and now I'm a man full of hope. You're that hope.

GABRIEL: Won't you come down?

DUNCAN: This is no place for truth telling.

[*He starts to climb down from the crows nest.* GABRIEL *lets him go first. He stops almost at once.*]

DUNCAN: I'm stuck.

GABRIEL: What?

DUNCAN: This pole. I can't stand heights.

[*He sways ominously and white knuckles the rail.*]

[GABRIEL *climbs round his body to get a grip on the other side of the ladder.*]

GABRIEL: We'll go down together.

DUNCAN: Very romantic.

[*She smiles at him tenderly. Ruefully he smiles back and they begin to descend together* GABRIEL *watching him all the time.*]

GABRIEL: Just look at me and concentrate.

DUNCAN: If I look at you I won't be able to concentrate.

[*They continue down and make it to the bottom,* DUNCAN *breathes out heavily, he's sweating.* DR BEAD *gives him his jacket.* GABRIEL *goes ahead.* DUNCAN *follows, running a little to catch up. We hear their voices.*]

GABRIEL: I thought you were a man of the world.

DUNCAN: I was.

63. EXT. DECK. DAY 5

DUNCAN *is visible in the background taking photographs of various passengers on board, including* DR BEAD *and* MISS QUIM. GABRIEL *is standing on her own, a little way from the group, looking at a large board where other of* DUNCAN's *passenger photos are pinned up for display. There's a sign on the board which says* DUNCAN STEWART. PHOTOGRAPHER. GABRIEL *is looking particularly at a photo of herself with* DUNCAN. *It looks*

like a wedding pose, except for their clothes. As she looks REX
GOODYEAR *comes behind her. We hear his voice before* GABRIEL
sees him.

REX: They say the camera never lies but what about the
photographer?

[GABRIEL *wheels round and turns straight into* REX *whose
standing too close.*]

REX: I too have some photographs.

[*He flashes a small sheaf at* GABRIEL *and fans them out like a
hand of cards. They're old, worn, but the man in them,
sometimes by himself, sometimes with Rex's wife, could easily
be Duncan, although he is fair, where Duncan is dark.*]

REX: The resemblance is uncanny.

GABRIEL: Resemblances usually are . . . If you're so sure that
Duncan has your painting why don't you ask him for it?

REX: I'm not sure. You think me an unfeeling man don't you
Gabriel? And perhaps I am these days but I have only ever
loved two things, my pictures and my wife. Alasdair Birch took
them both.

GABRIEL: You said your wife was murdered.

[REX *simply holds out the photo of his wife and the* DUNCAN-
MAN GABRIEL *realises that he's citing Duncan as the
murderer. She turns and runs away.*]

[GABRIEL *runs into the nearest lower deck door.*]

63A. INT. CORRIDOR. DAY 5

GABRIEL *runs down the corridor, through another door.*

63B. EXT. DECK. DAY 5

GABRIEL *runs onto the deck and comes past the map. As she comes
to the map* REX *is watching for her. Solid, silent, threatening.*

GABRIEL: I don't believe Duncan killed your wife.

REX: Belief has nothing to do with it. When you discover the truth
you must live with it. Her body was washed up on the shores of
Brittany. She and Birch had planned to settle in France, the

romantic rural life. She was found dead and Birch was not found at all.

GABRIEL: You've no proof that Duncan is this man.

[*She turns as if to go. Rex's words lasso her back. As soon as he says 'police' she turns round again.*]

REX: I dare say the police could get to the bottom of our identity crisis. Would you like me to tell the Captain of my suspicions? That we have a murderer on board sharing a cabin with his supposed wife? [*he laughs*] No, I am a man of the world and I will give you a chance. Both of you. Get me the painting, the real painting, and the man you love will never see me again.

[*He holds out his hands rather as* DUNCAN *did earlier.*]

GABRIEL: I don't love him.

[REX *watches her move away, slowly this time.*]

64. INT. CORRIDORS. DAY 5

GABRIEL *heads back to her own cabin, down towards D22. She passes two black maids leaning on a big laundry basket. They're dealing Tarot cards. One of them pushes the pack towards* GABRIEL. *She cuts it, turns over the Tower.*

65. INT. FLASHBACK. VESUVIA'S HUT. CARIBBEAN. NIGHT

A fire in the corner. The room is lit with flares.

GABRIEL *and* VESUVIA *are sitting opposite one another on the floor.*

VESUVIA *is dealing Tarot cards.*

VESUVIA: I see your future here Gabriel. The fool, a new beginning, Six of Swords, travel with difficulty to a foreign land. The Lovers, that must be you and Michael. The Nine of Swords, heartbreak and pain. The Ace of Cups, love again, a gift from the sky, a mystery, a dream.

[VESUVIA *pushes the pack over to* GABRIEL.]

[GABRIEL *cuts the pack. She gets the Tower.*]

[*She holds it up to* VESUVIA.]

66. INT. CABIN D22. DAY 5.

VESUVIA: [*V.O.*] The Tower, Dissolution, change, loss. The safe walls are falling child.

[GABRIEL *opens the door of her cabin and sits wearily on the bottom bunk. She feels something hard under the covers. She fiddles about and pulls out the gun and opens the magazine. It's loaded. As she does so she hears* VESUVIA'*s voice ending the previous flashback.*]

67. EXT. THE SWIMMING POOL. DAY 5.

The weather is bright and clear.

DR BEAD *is swimming up and down the pool in sedate lengths. Other* PASSENGERS *sit round the side.*

A STEWARD *buzzes about with drinks.*

MISS QUIM *is at the pool edge, swimming costume on, her feet in the water. She's making handwritten alterations to her play 'The Temptation'.*

The BLACK STEWARD *puts a record on the poolside turntable. It's 'Happy Talk' from South Pacific.*

DR BEAD *swims into* MISS QUIM'*s range.*

MISS QUIM: Damned if I know how this thing should end Angela.

DR BEAD: Shouldn't it have a moral ending?

MISS QUIM: Why?

DR BEAD: Because it's about temptation.

MISS QUIM: I've got to the part where the angel imprisoned in the tower is about to go with Satan to his boudoir. What shall we do after that?

DR BEAD: His boudoir? Satan's boudoir? Boudoir?

MISS QUIM: It's French.

[GABRIEL *appears at the pool in her swimwear. Towel round her neck. She looks tired.*

DR BEAD: It's nonsense in any language. Hello Gabriel, do excuse me, I have to think of my butterfly.

[*She swims elegantly away, butterfly stroke.*]

GABRIEL: Have you ever fallen in love?

MISS QUIM: Yes my dear.

GABRIEL: And did it take you by surprise?

MISS QUIM: There is no other way to be taken.

[DR BEAD *returns her length. Stands up and stretches her arms. She's intent on her swimming, not* MISS QUIM *and* GABRIEL.]

GABRIEL: [*nodding*] Duncan told me you and Dr Bead are lesbians. I knew you were happy together. But I didn't know the word . . . it seems so easy for you, it's obvious that you love one another but it's not obvious that Duncan loves me. I wanted to ask you whether. . . .

[*She realises that* DR BEAD *and* MISS QUIM *are staring at her thunderstruck.*]

[DR BEAD'*s arms are stuck up in the air.*]

DR BEAD: Gwen and I have never had a physical relationship.

MISS QUIM: No, no, no, absolutely not. Held hands, yes, little peck on the cheek at cocoa-time . . . little hug . . . little hug, when was that? On my birthday three years ago . . .

[*While* DR BEAD *is reciting her litany* DUNCAN *strolls up fully clothed.*]

DUNCAN: Ladies, what a lovely afternoon for it.

[DR BEAD *takes* DUNCAN *by the ankles and flips him belly flop into the pool.*]

[*She climbs out and walks away with great dignity.*]

[MISS QUIM *smiles at* GABRIEL *and pulls a face, gestures with her hands and scurries up the steps after* DR BEAD.]

[DUNCAN *comes spluttering to the surface.*]

DUNCAN: What did I say?

GABRIEL: Try lesbians.

[DUNCAN *turns bright red.*]

DUNCAN: Oh my God, Oh Lord, Gabriel, how could you? It was a joke, they're missionaries, Oh Gabriel.

GABRIEL: A joke? How much of what you tell me is a joke? Or I mean a lie?

[*She leaps in and swims swiftly to the other end of the pool.* DUNCAN *tries to swim after her.*]

[REX *appears in his smart swimwear. Slips in and swims in his own lane away from Duncan and Gabriel.*]

DUNCAN: Give me another chance Gabriel. I tried to tell you everything last night but I couldn't do it.

[REX *swims deftly across to* GABRIEL'*s free side.*]

REX: Perhaps you've had time to think about our bargain?

DUNCAN: Gabriel, let's get out now.

[GABRIEL *kicks under the water. She swims with her eyes open. She can see* REX's *legs opening and shutting in a sedate breaststroke.*]

[DUNCAN *kicks frenetically along.*]

[GABRIEL's *hearing* DUNCAN *and* REX's *voices, distorted, menacing.*]

REX: I only wanted to help you Miss Angel.

DUNCAN: The walls are falling away Gabriel.

REX: No proof but the police could resolve ... police could resolve.

DUNCAN: I am Duncan Stewart. Trust me Gabriel, Gabriel ...

REX: Truth has nothing to do with belief, Miss Angel.

DUNCAN: Truth or Dare?

REX: Get me the painting. The painting. The painting.

[GABRIEL *shoots up from under water as if she's being pressure powered. She climbs out of the pool and walks away.*]

[REX *swims sedately on.*]

[DUNCAN *scrambles after her.*]

68. INT. CABIN D22. LATER. DAY 5

The Modesty Changing Rail is strung across the cabin.

Split screen: on one side we can see GABRIEL *naked for a second then pulling on a dry dress.*

On the other side DUNCAN *is taking off his wet clothes.*

GABRIEL: Did you kill Rex Goodyear's wife?

DUNCAN: We were out in a little boat. I tried to stop her jumping off to swim but she wasn't the sort of woman a man can stop. It took the sea to do that.

GABRIEL: Why didn't you go to the police?

DUNCAN: I thought they'd be suspicious. I was afraid. Can't you understand that? I've never been a criminal Gabriel but I'm the sort of man the police like to keep an eye on.

GABRIEL: Because you're a forger?

DUNCAN: You make me sound like a spiv with a line of five-pound notes.

[*Suddenly he unhooks the rail. He's naked.* GABRIEL *looks at him in disbelief. He steps towards her tentatively. She steps back.*]

DUNCAN: I wanted to show you that I've nothing to hide.

GABRIEL: Can I believe any of this?

DUNCAN: Can't you believe what you see?

[GABRIEL *moves towards him, touches him gently on his chest and runs her hands down his arm. Carefully he kisses her head. Then lifts up her face towards him. Kisses her fully. She holds him.*]

[*He kneels down in front of her, wraps his arms around her knees. She massages his shoulders. He runs his hands up her legs, pushing up her dress.*]

[*They make love.*]

69. INT. BAR. DAY 6. MORNING

DUNCAN *and* GABRIEL *are in the bar.*

He pops a magnum of champagne, spills it down himself, pours for GABRIEL.

She drinks, sneezes, spills it down herself.

70. INT. CABIN D22. DAY 6

DUNCAN *in full kilt rig is standing behind* GABRIEL *showing her how to blow the bagpipes. The bag swells up and up to bursting size,* GABRIEL's *cheeks swell up and up to bursting size. No sound.*

71. EXT. DECK. DAY 6

DUNCAN *and* GABRIEL *are on deck. It's sunny.*

He's photographing her in different poses.

She takes the camera, photographs him, he puts his hands over his face.

72. EXT. BOAT DECK. DAY 6. NIGHT

DUNCAN *and* GABRIEL *are in the lifeboat under the tarpaulin making love.*

They climb out. It's night.

They walk arm in arm to the deck rail. Up above, the moon, the stars.

Behind, in the shadows, REX GOODYEAR, *watching.*

73. INT. FIRST CLASS CORRIDOR. DAY 7

DUNCAN *is standing outside Rex Goodyear's cabin.*

He knocks. No response.

DUNCAN *knocks again and puts on a Jamaican accent.*

DUNCAN: Mistah Goodyeeur? Mistah Goodyeeur? You there please?

[*No response.*]

[DUNCAN *gets out an impressive skeleton tool and deftly picks the lock.*]

73A. INT. REX'S CABIN. DAY 7

DUNCAN *goes in and looks around. Rex's folder of cuttings is spread out on the bed. The offending photo lies on top.* DUNCAN *pockets the photo then starts sifting through the cuttings.*

74. EXT. PURSERS OFFICE. DAY 7

GABRIEL *comes out of the Purser's office carrying a hefty sheaf of papers. She's troubled.* REX GOODYEAR *suddenly looms up out of a deck chair where he's been sitting. She gives a little cry.*

GABRIEL: Duncan didn't kill your wife. It was an accident.

REX: Oh he told you that did he? Thank you. At least we agree we're talking about the same man.

[GABRIEL *realises what she has done.* REX *now has the upper hand.* GABRIEL *tries to move past him.*]

REX: It's rather difficult to stab yourself in the back.

GABRIEL: What? You said she was washed up on the beach.

REX: Oh she was. But it wasn't death by water. She was already dead when she was thrown *into* the water.

[REX *turns and leaves.* GABRIEL *drops her sheaf of papers. They scatter and start to blow about the deck.*]

[*The* BLACK STEWARD *rushes over and starts trying to collect them up.*]

STEWARD: Please Miss, don't be upset about these papers. Everyone has to fill in immigration papers. Everyone like us.

[*He stands and hands her a messy bundle.*]

STEWARD: It's simple, you just fill in each set 5 times.

[GABRIEL *can't speak. She looks at the* STEWARD *through a sea of pain.*]

[*The* STEWARD *misunderstands. He speaks gently to her.*]

STEWARD: Miss, it's all right for you. You got a husband, a white husband, an address, money, a place to go. Most of the girls I see got nothing and they're going to nothing. Me, I can't get off this ship, just to steady my legs, no papers.

[*He points to the bundle.*]

STEWARD: You should be glad of them papers.

[*She looks at the papers pointlessly.*]

75. INT. THE BAR. DAY 7

DUNCAN *is sitting in the bar by himself. Whisky beside him.*

DUNCAN'S *carving an ethnic looking doll from a piece of wood. He uses a curved well looked after knife. He's skilled. He's whistling 'Happy Talk'.*

GABRIEL *comes through the bar on the opposite side, carrying the papers. Doesn't see* DUNCAN. *She's clearly preoccupied.*

He sees her, half rises, then thinks better of it.

76. INT. CORRIDORS. APPROACHING D22. DAY 7

GABRIEL *is on her way to the cabin.*

77. INT. D22. DAY 7

GABRIEL *takes out Duncan's gun and empties the bullets. She puts it back where she found it. Exits.*

[*No Scene 78 – CUT*]

79. INT. MISS QUIM'S CABIN. DAY 7

MISS QUIM *is typing furiously in her smashed cabin.* DR BEAD *is standing behind her holding the script.* MISS QUIM *stops and swivels round.*

MISS QUIM: I had to tell you everything Angela. You can see why the poor girl's confused.

DR BEAD: Women and men. I often think it's God's little joke. She should forget about both of them.

MISS QUIM: She's in love Angela.

DR BEAD: It's very bad for the blood pressure.

[GABRIEL *comes barging in. She's in a state.*]

GABRIEL: Professor Goodyear came to me just now. He said his wife didn't drown. He said she was stabbed in the back. Did Duncan do that?

[DR BEAD *and* MISS QUIM *look at one another in horror.* MISS QUIM *jumps up and hugs* GABRIEL. DR BEAD *quickly looks outside the cabin door then locks it.*]

MISS QUIM: Calm down Gabriel. There may be nothing in this story at all.

DR BEAD: The Professor might be lying.

GABRIEL: What if Duncan's the one who's lying?

MISS QUIM: We shall have to make a plan.

DR BEAD: [*looking at her watch*] We're due to see Mr Stewart for rehearsal in twenty minutes.

MISS QUIM: You'll have to confront him Gabriel. It's the only way.

GABRIEL: He's got a gun.

[*She opens her hand to reveal the bullets.* DR BEAD *draws a sharp intake of breath. She puts a hand on* GABRIEL's *shoulder.*]

MISS QUIM: Oh he has, has he? Well we won't worry about that my dear. He's not the only one.

[*She crosses to the closet and pulls out a huge double-barrelled shotgun.* DR BEAD *looks delighted.* GABRIEL *is rather appalled.*]

80. EXT. DECK. DAY 7

DUNCAN *is on deck with his script. He's got the script on his knees but he's carving an ethnic-looking doll with a cruel-bladed knife.*

He's swift and sure. He can handle the knife. GABRIEL *comes towards him. She sees the knife.*

DUNCAN *smiles and says directly to* GABRIEL:

DUNCAN: Your face is a lantern
Held high above my heart.
My heart is a dark place
Tented against the light.
Light the narrow passage
Of desire. Light the well
Where love is drowned.
Love leaps
To your sight as summer leaps
To sun leaps to light.

[*He gazes at* GABRIEL *very tenderly. She doesn't know how to respond.*]

[GABRIEL *pulls herself together.*]

GABRIEL: What are you doing with that knife?

DUNCAN: That's not in the script. I'm making you a lucky charm. A friend for all weathers.

GABRIEL: I thought that was you.

[DUNCAN *laughs and takes her arm. The knife in his other hand.*]

[*They walk across the deck.*]

DUNCAN: I have a little house in London. We could go there together. You're going to need a place to live.

GABRIEL: I have a place to live.

DUNCAN: I see.

GABRIEL: You think I should be happy to live in a house I've never seen in a place I've never been with a man I don't know?

DUNCAN: Get to know me. Ask me anything.

GABRIEL: How did Mrs Goodyear get stabbed in the back?

[DUNCAN's *face opens into recognition and fear.*]

[*He looks at the knife in his hand. He throws it over the side.*]

[GABRIEL *faces him steadily.*]

[DUNCAN *sighs.*]

DUNCAN: I've got something to show you.

81. INT. D22. DAY 7

A large oil painting, about five feet two is extended on a stretcher. Lucifer is being thrown out of the vault of Heaven for refusing to serve God. His wings are already tarnishing as he falls to earth. A female Angel is falling with him, holding him the way parachute divers do. It's wings are still bright.

GABRIEL *and* DUNCAN *are looking at it.*

DUNCAN: Ten years ago I made a bet with Rex's wife that the great God Goodyear couldn't tell the difference between a fake of mine and the real thing. It was this Titian we chose. You see this painting, this extraordinary painting had only just come on the market. It had been lost since 1560. That's a long time to be lost, even longer than me. I followed it around the world for a year, from exhibition to exhibition, drawing it, photographing it, reproducing it bit by bit. Finally, Rex got his hands on it to write a paper on the pigments and the glaze. With his wife's help, I swopped my copy for the original. Rex didn't notice. He wrote the paper, published it, and then I wrote to him and revealed all.

GABRIEL: Telling him you'd got this one?

DUNCAN: Yes, oh and by then I'd got his wife too. You see I won my bet.

GABRIEL: She was your bet?

DUNCAN: You make it sound too crude.

[GABRIEL *raises her eyebrows at him and thinks.*]

GABRIEL: Why did you kill her?

DUNCAN: [*angry*] I didn't kill her. Do you hear me Gabriel? I didn't kill her. [*his voice softens*] Look at me . . .

[DUNCAN *takes* GABRIEL *by the shoulders and turns her to him. She doesn't want to look at him.*]

DUNCAN: I never wanted to involve you in any of this. I'm the loser Gabriel, not you. A loser but not a murderer. She drowned. I know she drowned.

[*It's Duncan's turn to look away. He is agitated.* GABRIEL *moves away from him towards the wall that adjoins D22 with Dr Bead's cabin.*]

GABRIEL: Are you Alasdair Birch?

DUNCAN: He's dead too and that's official. I have his death certificate. The ultimate fake I suppose. Poor Duncan Stewart is the only one alive who can tell you the truth. [*This is rather sinister*].

GABRIEL: And Rex Goodyear.

[*She looks* DUNCAN *full in the face.*]

GABRIEL: If you're telling me the truth then give him his painting.

DUNCAN: Is that your price?

GABRIEL: I can't be bought.

DUNCAN: No. [*he pauses*] I have held in my hands some of the most precious things in the world but none so lovely as your face.

[DUNCAN *goes over to her and takes her face in his hands. She looks at him anxiously, searchingly. He looks at her with great tenderness. She wants to believe him. He kisses her softly. She kisses him back more fiercely. He moves to put her back against the wall. She slips and thuds against it.* DUNCAN *scoops her down onto the floor and opens her dress.*]

GABRIEL: Duncan, no, wait . . . DUNCAN . . .

[DUNCAN *takes no notice. The door flies open and* DR BEAD *and* MISS QUIM *come in.*]

[MISS QUIM *has her shotgun.*]

[DR BEAD *a large copy of the Bible.*]

DR BEAD: Leave that young woman alone. I am a magistrate.

[*She waves her Bible at* DUNCAN. *Goes forward and hits him over the head with it.*]

[*He passes out.*]

MISS QUIM: Well done Angela. The Bible still packs a punch I'm glad to say.

DR BEAD: It's my steel-plated emergency Bible.

[MISS QUIM *puts her foot on* DUNCAN'*s chest and points the gun at him.*]

GABRIEL: He didn't do it. It was Professor Goodyear.

MISS QUIM: But you banged the wall and your dress is open.

[GABRIEL *hurriedly covers herself and gets some water for* DUNCAN *while she's talking.*]

GABRIEL: I slipped. He was kissing me. You see . . .

DR BEAD: He's not your husband.

GABRIEL: No, but I am married.

DR BEAD and MISS QUIM: What?!

GABRIEL: To someone else. His name's Michael.

DR BEAD: Perhaps it's time for the whole truth my dear. We'll be next door.

82. INT. MISS QUIM'S CABIN. DAY 7. EVENING

DR BEAD *and* MISS QUIM *are sitting in the deepening gloom of the evening. They have made several pots of tea. Sense of time having passed.*

MISS QUIM: So you see Angela, I have loved you with all my heart all my life. From the first moment I saw you. Your hair was cut in a bob then and when you bent to read a book your hair fell slightly and hid your face. I never wanted your face to be hid.

DR BEAD: For thirty two years you've kept this secret?

MISS QUIM: I had to.

DR BEAD: First you tell me you only joined the missionary service because you couldn't get a job with Thomas Cook. Now you tell me that for thirty two years you've felt for me the way a man feels for a woman?

MISS QUIM: No Angela. I love you the way a woman loves a woman. It's quite different.

DR BEAD: Were you glad when I didn't marry Jonney?

MISS QUIM: Handlebar Jonney, the man and his moustache. Do you remember how he used to come to our college and you and I would be ready to spend the day together working or off on our bicycles and he'd say . . . [*she impersonates him*] 'Move over Gwen. Let the dog see the rabbit'.

DR BEAD: Yes . . . he didn't have a way with words did he? What did he have?

MISS QUIM: A moustache.

[MISS QUIM *and* DR BEAD *laugh.*]

[MISS QUIM *leans forward. Their knees touch.*]

MISS QUIM: At least you gave him up for Jesus.

DR BEAD: Not quite. I gave him up for you.

MISS QUIM: What?

DR BEAD: I preferred your company. We were better friends, we were closer partners. You used to put your arm around me and I liked that. I didn't make the leap into thinking that you and I could be . . . should be . . .

MISS QUIM: Lovers?

DR BEAD: Lovers.

[*She says the word as if it's new to her.*]

DR BEAD: I didn't have the courage Gwen. It takes courage not to do the obvious thing but to do the right thing.

MISS QUIM: I've been no better. [*pauses*] Look Angela, you've always said that a signal of God's grace is that people get a second chance. God or not, this is our chance. Don't buy that little bungalow by yourself. Let's buy a big farmhouse together.

DR BEAD: And keep hens. I've always wanted hens.

MISS QUIM: And have a cat.

DR BEAD: And a dog called Rover. And plenty of rooms where people can stay.

MISS QUIM: We don't know anybody.

DR BEAD: We will.

[MISS QUIM *leaps up and surveys the top bunk.*]

MISS QUIM: Help me get that mattress down will you? We can put them both side by side.

DR BEAD: [*realising*] Side by side?

[MISS QUIM *moves forward and kisses her very tenderly.*]

MISS QUIM: On the floor.

DR BEAD: What about my back?

MISS QUIM: What about your heart?

[MISS QUIM *and* DR BEAD *touch one another, tentative, amazed, then passionate.*]

83. INT. THE BOWELS OF THE SHIP

DUNCAN *is standing alone looking at the painting in a roll in his hands. He holds it closely to him. He looks ahead deep in thought. A man doing something difficult a man doing something that he wants to do but that still represents a sacrifice. A man resolute but hurting.* REX *appears behind him. We see both their faces.* REX's *impassive.* DUNCAN's *thoughtful, vulnerable expression hardening as he realises that* REX *is behind him. He turns swiftly and holds out his hand.*

DUNCAN: Alasdair Birch. Pleased to meet you.

REX: [*Ignoring his hand*] I've come for my painting.

[REX *smiles contemptuously at* DUNCAN.]

DUNCAN: I've come for my life.

REX: I wasn't aware that you had one.

DUNCAN: For the last nine years I've been a dead man Professor. A man without hope. I got on this ship to find another of my kind, the only other dead man I know. I came after you and I found Gabriel Angel. A woman with the life so bright in her that she made me see myself as I am. . . .

REX: A forger, an adulterer, a liar.

DUNCAN: And as I could be. Once before I put an obsession in the way of love. [*He raises the painting*] And I kept the obsession and I lost the love. I won't do it this time. Take your painting. [*He throws it across at* REX. *It bangs against the wall.* REX *struggles to get it. It's torn a little.* REX *is furious.*]

REX: You fool. You'd destroy the most precious thing in the world.

DUNCAN: I never even raised my voice to her.

[REX *scrambles up with the painting. He's lost his superior composure.*]

REX: You killed her. Your knife killed her.

DUNCAN: We both killed her. My knife, your blow. The blow that was meant for me. That's what happens isn't it? Men fight and women get killed. I go back to that place again and again, the water, the boat, the painting, the knife. My best love can't change it even for a day but love can change now; this water, this boat, the painting, the knife.

[*He takes it out of his pocket and throws it at* REX's *feet. He turns and leaves.*]

85. EXT. DECK. DAY 8. EVENING

GABRIEL *walks through the crowds. She's wearing her flying jacket.*

The deck is hung with balloons and streamers. The jazz band are playing dance tunes.

A makeshift stage has been erected. A couple of jugglers are on stage juggling. There's a sign that says 9pm The Temptation. We see parts of people's bodies as they dance: feet, hands, hips. It's reminiscent of the dockside at the beginning.

Some guests wear masks.

DUNCAN *comes by in full kilt gear. He comes behind* GABRIEL *and takes off her flying jacket. Puts it on the stage. She turns round. He kisses her.*

GABRIEL: There's something I want to tell you.

DUNCAN: I thought you had no secrets.

[DR BEAD *and* MISS QUIM *come over.* DR BEAD *is in her Fortuny dress. She has all her jewellery on and a flattering amount of make-up. She looks exquisite.* MISS QUIM *holds her arm. They are both shining.*]

MISS QUIM: Secrets? Oh don't we all have a skeleton in the cupboard somewhere Mr Stewart.

DR BEAD: I like to think of them as family pets.

DUNCAN: Ladies . . . I was meaning to apologise . . . it was rude of me . . . I . . .

[*He's deeply embarrassed. The ladies rather enjoy this.*]

DR BEAD: As a medical lady Mr Stewart, I can tell you guilt will do you no good at all. And as a woman I can tell you that the best remedy for guilt is love.

[*She kisses him on the cheek.* DUNCAN *puts his hand to his cheek. He doesn't know what to do.* MISS QUIM *kisses him on the other cheek. He blushes and holds* GABRIEL's *hand tightly.*]

[DR BEAD *and* MISS QUIM *dance away, wrapped up in one another.*]

DUNCAN: I'm jealous.

[*He gazes after them with some admiration.*]

GABRIEL: There's something I have to tell you.

[DUNCAN *and* GABRIEL *move out of the throng hand in hand into the darker stern of the ship.*]

86. EXT. STERN OF SHIP. DAY 8. NIGHT

Near the Observation Pole there's a bonfire burning. It's eerie and primitive, the flames beat against the dark.

DUNCAN: There's something I want to show you.

[*He guides* GABRIEL *round a corner. She draws in her breath. There's a small bonfire blazing on deck. It's controlled, but rather shocking to find there, so sudden and dangerous.* DUNCAN *moves to a corner and brings out an armful of stuff, files, papers, bundles, photographs, and starts chucking them onto the fire.*]

DUNCAN: I'm going to give it to him myself. All this was my life. If you can call living in the past a life.

GABRIEL: It's about Michael.

DUNCAN: It's about Michael. I've only got two hands. I'll need them both if I'm going to hold on to you.

GABRIEL: Please listen.

DUNCAN: You're going to stay with him aren't you?

[*Angrily he chucks his last handful onto the fire. The photos of Rex's wife blaze up through the flames.*]

GABRIEL: There is no Michael.

[DUNCAN *stares at* GABRIEL *astonished.*]

GABRIEL: He's on his way back to Grenada. He won't be waiting at the docks with an armful of flowers.

DUNCAN: I thought I was the one with the surprises.

GABRIEL: He wrote to me every week for 2 years. He wrote in between scrubbing other people's floors, cleaning other people's toilets. He washed away their vomit and he wiped up their mess. That was his share of the dream. All he saved was enough money to come back home. I'd saved enough money to take me away. Do you see?

DUNCAN: No, no, why are you going to a place without hope?

GABRIEL: The hope's not in the place it's in me. I've left my family, I've left my home. I've taken everything that's Gabriel and put her on this boat. We're dreamin' people my people. Thomas's dream got him off the ground and he chased it across the sky until the sky took him. You have to risk the best you've got if you want a little bit of life.

[DUNCAN's *face. He knows this.*]

GABRIEL: I want my life. Not Thomas's, not Vesuvia's not Michael's, not my ancestors. All I can do is walk my own road and maybe fly some of the way [*she pauses*] even if I never get that aeroplane.

[*She smiles in recognition of that. It doesn't matter now.*]

DUNCAN: Can I come if I bring my own wings?

[*She laughs and holds him. It's a tender moment, very close and together.*]

[REX *steps out of the shadow.*]

REX: Very touching.

[DUNCAN *whirls round.* GABRIEL *is frightened.*]

DUNCAN: What do you want?

REX: I forgot to give you this. It's yours.

[*He waves the painting at* DUNCAN *then throws it onto the fire. The fire leaps up and begins to consume it immediately.* REX *laughs and laughs.* DUNCAN *is dumb struck for a moment. He tries to reach the painting but the heat is too fierce.* GABRIEL *pulls him back.* REX *is gleeful.*]

DUNCAN: Professor, don't you know that you had the real painting all the time . . . until tonight?

[REX *cries out like an animal.*]

[*At that moment a great cry comes from the party on the ship.*]

CROWD: Hooray, Hooray, Hooray.

[*A spate of fireworks etc.*]

DUNCAN: England. [*to* REX) If a painting's good it's good. What does it matter who painted it?

[DUNCAN *turns to* GABRIEL.]

[REX *slopes away.* DUNCAN *turns to* GABRIEL. GABRIEL *turns to camera to speak.*]

GABRIEL: This is where the story starts, stretched out in front of me, road like a runway heading for the blue sky. But the road bends and the sky's darker over there. I can't tell if I'm going into it or against it. What matters is that I go. In the Bible only the angels have wings, the rest of us have to learn how to leap.

ORANGES ARE NOT
THE ONLY FRUIT

AN INTRODUCTION IN FOUR ACTS

1. THE SCRIPTS*

A woman goes into an art gallery. She sees a vase and falls in love with it. She goes over to the sculptor and tells her how much she loves her work; the colour, the shape, the glaze, the particular wholeness of the piece. Naturally the sculptor is flattered. 'Yes', says the woman, getting out her cheque book, 'your work is unique. Now, could you just smash it up and make me six cups and saucers out of it?'

The first question for anyone transposing a book to the screen is how to smash up the original and do it justice in a different way. Faithful adaptations make bad television. It's better to have a new vision that is faithful to the spirit of the work, without worrying about fitting everything in, or even keeping the same order of events.

Time and place can be altered, if those elements are not crucial to the truth of the tale. For instance, it does no harm to play Shakespeare as you like it, but it would be unhelpful to take a novel about a mining community in Wales and set it in the Green Belt. A scriptwriter must be honest about any changes he or she makes. Do they work towards a perfect whole, or are the changes just a bit of tinkering? As the writer of both the novel and the scripts, I was not in the business of tinkering, but I knew that real changes had to be made to my experimental, in many ways anti-linear, novel to render it the kind of television that would bring

---

* Part of this section was first published in *Debut on Two: A Guide to Writing for Television*, edited by Phillippa Giles and Vicky Licorish, BBC Books, 1990.

viewers in off the streets. At the same time, I did not want to destroy at a stroke all the nuances, subtleties, games and cumulative effects that are the pleasures of well-written prose. I didn't want to lose anything and I wanted to gain a lot. What was to be done? My immediate task was to identify the difference between real losses and fond farewells. The fairy tales and allegorical passages that weave themselves within the main story could be waved goodbye without any pain because their function could be taken over by the camera itself. They worked as a kind of Greek Chorus commenting on the main events. The camera, with its silent ability to offer other dimensions to what appears to be happening, works as a mute Greek Chorus. The power of the image means that you don't always have to spell it out.

It was also necessary to decide what parts of the book were irrelevant to the story I had decided to tell on television. This is a question which dogs all scrupulous scriptwriters because a novel is often full of attendant passages which are not the story as such, but which are in themselves pleasurable. Inevitably some of these will have to go, if only so that the main theme can enjoy full development. Having done the hatchet work, the scriptwriter must try and heal the wounds by conveying along with the camera a sense of the scope of the original piece. In *Oranges*, I did my best to offer a consistently surreal world view to make up for the flights of fancy and the suggestiveness of language that I had felt could not be included. One of my favourite passages in the novel, a short essay on the differences between history and story-telling, entitled 'Deuteronomy', had to be left out. And yet it is central to the book and no accident that it falls precisely in the middle of the seven chapters. What I hope I have managed to do, is dissolve it and scatter it throughout the three episodes. The characters are always telling stories, to each other, about themselves, even to themselves, and set against this is the notion of history, objectivity, fact. In virtually every scene there are at least two definitions of reality at work. No single line is directed, though sympathies are suggested. What the viewer must do is to pick her way through this multiplicity of truth and time and decide what to believe. I think this properly conveys the simple though highly complex statement which is true of the book obliquely and that chapter very clearly; namely, I am lying to you but I am also telling you the truth. Trust me.

I didn't find it easy to break down my novel into three fifty-minute episodes, each complete in itself but leading temptingly to the next one. Naturally the ending of each had to be very strong. It's not alien to write a novel in this way, Dickens did it all the time, but if it's not your style, the transition presents problems. Very few books divide themselves neatly into same-length episodes and so a scriptwriter must be very careful to get the balance and pacing right. In many places I had to alter the sequence of events, stretch out some scenes, compress others and always be aware of the over-all emphasis I wanted. It's an obvious trap to fall into, when writing in parts, to concentrate on them as individual exercises and forget about the shape of the whole. Nevertheless, it is the whole on which we will be judged.

There is something fantastically artificial about trying to chop up a work with supermarket efficiency into nice same-sized chunks. It's not usually written or read that way. If it had been possible I would have preferred the episodes to have been different lengths; as it was I decided to accept the restrictions as a challenge and to see whether or not an internal time-rhythm could be set up that flouted the one I had been given.

Episode one is in respect of two and three quite leisurely. The characters are introduced without haste, without cramming, and we become accustomed to them and their habits without a great deal of 'action'. I don't overload the viewer with plot because I'm asking him or her to get to know my people. Once that's happened, I can fall into a kind of shorthand, the way we do with our friends, so that much can be transmitted by a little. My characters are not figures who act out a plot; they are the plot. Therefore it seemed right to weigh out the episodes differently, so that in the beginning we have enough room to know whom we're dealing with. This left the remaining episodes with a lot of ground to cover; the internal rhythm speeds up and intensifies until the very end of episode three, when a sudden slowing down creates a poignancy that is not only what the camera is doing or what the words are doing, but what the structure itself has made possible.

It is vital, then, when considering how to divide up the material you have chosen to include, to give serious attention to the internal time-rhythm and how it can contribute to the effect you are aiming for. It is a much more subliminal device than the others we are thinking about but just as powerful. Thirty minutes or fifty minutes a week is what you've got, but how you use it, how you stretch it or shrink it, is up to you. I believe, too, that concentration on the internal time-rhythm gets round the problem of sacrificing the depth of a novel to its pace. In my blackest hours, before I really hit on how to weight the thing, I felt like a hack porn writer who must put in a bit of sex every ten pages. Of course the thing has to be kept moving and above all we don't want our audience going off to make a cup of tea because they think nothing's going on, but movement doesn't mean action every moment. Let's not forget that art is about space.

What about language? So often the neglected sister of the big brother, the image. Words are my passion and I didn't want the dialogue of *Oranges* to sound like so much television-speak (and film-speak, to be fair). By that, I mean the dreary naturalism that is usually interpreted as realism. Naturalism and realism need not be the same thing. Harold Pinter and Alan Bennett both use highly artificial dialogue, sentences and shapes of sentences that one never encounters in real life, and yet their work is realistic in that it reflects common situations and reveals human emotions. Too many writers, in all media, struggle for realism and all they get is naturalism; flat, unapproachable situations, language so long dead it doesn't even smell anymore. For the screenwriter, that is a serious problem, especially since we have more than a sneaking suspicion that the audience only wants the pictures anyway.

But we cut our own throats. If we don't give them anything worth listening to, why should they listen? Most television drama and indeed most films could still be accompanied by the piano only, and no one would be any worse off. We have to find a language that is vibrant. A language that is the equal partner of the image. When adapting a work that does not depend on dialogue for its effects, the temptation is to overwrite; to shove into the mouth of any vaguely suitable character the impressions and persuasions that have been achieved in the novel by other means. It is usually better to let the camera stand in for those other means and to keep the dialogue free from weights it cannot bear. I do not mean by this that dialogue is a frivolous device unable to handle important material, but the flow of conversation must be precisely that: a flow, not a jam of information fighting for air.

We live in a society where more has become interchangeable with better, and we see this as much in writing as we do in the individual's determination to have everything, even if she doesn't want it. More words don't of themselves mean more power. A few words, perfectly placed, can have precisely the effect a writer wants; tears, laughter, a sudden shift of sympathy. I'm not advocating great tracts of silence, simply urging us to consider what the words are doing and whether we're using them well. In television or film, sloppy language is as unacceptable as sloppy camerawork, though the latter seems to worry people more.

My own solution to the problem of over-writing, a problem which persisted in some areas, even after I had identified what the camera could do without any help from me, was to keep the exchanges between characters unnaturally short. No one watching casually will notice this technique, namely my remarks about naturalism and realism, but it works very well and makes certain that nothing is made too obvious or too tedious. Even in long scenes the movement from one character to the other or others is rapid. I don't leave room for any of them to use words they don't need. They are to the point without seeming spartan. Whenever I wrote a scene, I went back over it and took away redundancy and excess. I do this continually in my novel-writing and it seemed proper to take such pains with dialogue, where the relative monotony of having only one major literary device at my disposal sometimes made me careless. Short exchanges have a further bonus; should you choose to depart from that technique for a while, the effect of a soliloquy or a few longueurs is greatly heightened. The change of rhythm adds to the power of the moment you wish to stand out.

Radio drama, very satisfactory in its own right, is excellent training for scriptwriters. Adaptations are usually first-rate and much can be learned from reading the work in question, then carefully investigating why the adaptation is a success. What techniques are being used and could they transfer to the screen?

On the radio, there are no pictures, except for the ones the words can create in the listener's imagination. This makes it an exacting medium and one where any verbal insecurity is immediately obvious. It is interesting to note that the presence of a narrator in most adaptations is designed to free the dialogue from unnecessary drag in much the same way as the camera does on screen.

What can we expect from language? Everything. Just as there are no bad dogs, only bad trainers, so there is no bad language, only bad writers. Why devise language at all? To communicate. To communicate what? Shopping list needs and directions and advice about the weather are soon soaked up by a very few words and the rudiments of grammar. So what are we to do with the richness that remains? Ignore it? Neglect it? Or ride it like a racehorse through every kind of country? The more we ask of language, the more we shall receive. I think it is incumbent upon any scriptwriter to use language well; to recognise that if the script itself is powerful, without any of the benefits of actors and director and all the alchemy that takes place on set, the finished product is likely to be outstanding. This matters. We do not need any more mediocre television.

Please do not misunderstand me; all of the arts are suffering from a bad bout of mediocrity. Television, uncertain of its own credentials and forced to fill up a blank screen every moment of the day and night, is bound to suffer more than the less-pressed custodians of culture. If television is here to stay, and it seems to be, we must demand of it the very best possible as often as possible. That means demanding of ourselves, as scriptwriters, the very best. The script should be the foundation of the finished product, not the rough guide or endlessly reworked blueprint, sometimes so endlessly reworked that it bears no resemblance to what the writer had in mind. A 'so-so' script just begs to be treated in an offhand manner; if it's full of holes, then the only person who'll fall through them is the writer. Meanwhile, the director and the cast will sew it up between them.

Ideally, of course, there will be complete collaboration between workers on the team and that has certainly been my experience. However, I've talked to other writers whose experience has not been anything like as harmonious and whose presence has been viewed as 'a necessary evil'. I do believe that a strong script makes that impossible. Our job is to make the most triumphant thing we can and then step back to allow the director and cast and all the great machine to bring their vision to it. We can't expect them to cover up for our inadequacies.

This brings us to our next point of discussion, the process of shooting the scripts and the position of the scriptwriter within that process.

2. THE FILMING

Novelists are solo pilots. As a scriptwriter I had managed to get used to the constant input of the director, Beeban Kidron, and the producer, Phillippa Giles, but I was not prepared for the sudden influx of a cast of 25-plus and as many technicians, all armed with a marked-up copy of my script.

The most curious thing for me, as a story-teller, was finding that a written text, once dramatised, generates new stories of its own; in other words it returns to its most ancient form, the oral tradition. Just as Scheherazade begins the *Thousand and One Nights* with a simple tale that becomes the mother of all the other tales, so the actors in *Oranges* began telling each other, and me, stories about their characters. They were inventing pasts and futures for themselves as well as following the written present on the page. It was a lesson in subjectivity; nothing is final, no text ever finishes, there is no last word, no summing up, there are only guesses and conjectures and games. I have already said that art is about space – the space to go on making things up, the freedom we feel once outside the prisons of our own experience. Art is always leading somewhere else, redefining itself and us as time passes, showing up the nonsense of objectivity. There is no such thing as a set text. For me, having rewritten a work that was in itself a rewriting of my life, I was struck by the schizophrenia I felt as soon as we began filming. It was no longer my life we were dealing with, except in the remotest sense, but it was my story. I had told a story to myself about myself and now other people were telling it back to me. Not only telling it back to me but wanting changes along the way.

The close work that was done with the script during the early days of shooting was a response to the actors settling into their roles, fleshing them out, and sometimes, therefore, highlighting omissions or incongruities. A few things disappeared, others gained extra weight. Throughout, there are little ad libs, lines I might have written but didn't, that came quite naturally from the characters because the characters have become themselves. Actor and role have fused. I wasn't present on the set very often, largely because Beeban thought I might be a disruptive figure for the actors. It's too easy for actors to check their readings against the facts when a piece does have discernable roots in life. But, by the filming stage, there were very few facts left and none I could offer up that would have been much help. *Oranges* is not autobiography and the only authenticity was the one we were inventing. We all recognised this but there was a chance that precious time would be lost by forgetting it now and then. Also my presence seemed to make some of the actors nervous.

The most extraordinary part of the filming was the fairground sequence that opens episodes one and three. When I decided to leave out the fairy-tale elements of the novel for the reasons discussed in the previous section, I wanted something else that would signal very strongly, right from the start, that this was no ordinary kitchen-sink drama. I chose a steam fair. The opening shot of *Oranges* shows Jess in both her incarnations, as played by Emily Aston and Charlotte Coleman, walking hand in hand towards a brightly lit, slightly shimmering fairground. It looks like a dream, soon to become a nightmare. It is both arresting and terrifying.

It was a night-shoot and we were due to start at about 10 p.m., after supper. The fair had been sited on a disused airfield outside Elstree and I hadn't been given directions in time. I set off, driving out through busy built-up north London and eventually passing into the sudden and surprising dark-green space beyond. Crossing the M1 was more like going over a moat than a motorway – I looked in the mirror and there was no more London. Only night-time and nothing. Then I saw a huge ferris wheel turning slowly in the distance. Repeatedly I tried to turn the car in the right direction; repeatedly I got lost, only to see the wheel looming again in another place. Eventually I threw my car outside the firmly locked gates of what I assumed to be the airfield and climbed over. After a rough short cut through some bushes and a bank of rabbits I saw the fair ahead of me, glittering across a level plain. I walked towards it and there was no-one there; the cast and crew were still eating in the trailers. Then I saw Charlotte Coleman, dressed as Jess, sitting by herself in one of the dodgem cars. Where was I that night? In the car or out of it? Myself or that other self made by me but no less real? It was windy and the swing boats creaked. An airfield at night, a deserted fairground visible for miles. Me or not me or both of me? I have always dealt in the imagination but now I could touch it, walk through it. I had typed 'Steam Fair' and the words had become flesh.

And then it was all over; the fair, the filming, the trailers full of costumes, the catering tables laden with sandwiches at tea-time. The actors were gone, but for Beeban another challenge was just beginning – the cutting room.

3. THE FILM

The filming of *Oranges* took about 3 months. For Beeban and her film editor, John Strickland, the task ahead was an enormous one; the offer of a screening at the London Film Festival on 26 November 1989 gave us a little less than half the time it would normally take at the BBC to prepare a project the size of *Oranges*. The festival was particularly important because we had worked hard to attract the director's (Sheila Whittaker) interest in it and because it is extremely prestigious for a TV series to be given that kind of serious film-goers' critical space. We knew, too, that being included would raise our profile within the BBC. *Oranges* had never hidden its light under a bushel and we were always encouraged by the Head of Drama, Mark Shivas, but we were still an unknown quantity. Beeban had not worked on anything similar before, Phillippa Giles had never produced before and it was my first attempt at screen writing. Add to that our rather low age rating – all under 30 at the time of commission – and it's easy to see why we needed a few boosts from the industry itself.

Beeban had always started her day at around 6.30 a.m. and finished 12 hours or so later, now she stepped up her performance to finish at midnight and expected everyone else she needed to do the same. They did. From start to finish *Oranges* attracted extraordinary loyalty and commitment from those who chose to work on it. People saw it as something special and that's partly why it became so.

I had written too much, no question of it. We had under-estimated the lengths of some of the scenes and now we were faced with the difficult task of further editing. We had pared it down beautifully at the script stage, would we now have to mutilate it?

Fortunately I was not involved in this process at all. Had I not been working with a director whom I trusted implicitly and respected enormously, I don't think I could have coped with my occasional nightmares about the cutting-room floor. But at last it was ready for me to see. The music hadn't been put on and the opening fairground sequences weren't in place but the body of the work was there. To begin with it was a terrible day. A woman had a baby on the Central Line and I was desperately late getting to Ealing Studios. The producer, Phillippa Giles, was waiting for me, we were both nervous, although matters were slightly improved by Emma Thompson who had thoughtfully armed me with a packet of popcorn from Hollywood. I knew that most writers usually hate the finished product, at best it doesn't offend them too much. I loved *Oranges* – the performances, the costumes, the locations and Beeban's perfect shots. It was much bigger, much more than I had ever imagined. For the first time I began to see what is possible when people of equal vision and like minds pool their resources. It was not an adaptation of my novel – it had become a work of art in its own right and only part of that process was me.

I knew that script inside out; I had lived with it for 18 months by the time I saw it on the screen. It was as though I was there for the first time, with no connections, no prior knowledge. Now that I can pinpoint the cuts accurately, I wonder why the material was there in the first place. Even if we had left it all in it would have been different but not better. So much can be left unsaid. As a novelist that was anathema to me. We found we had told our story in so many words but also in so many spaces. Art is about space.

4. THE RESPONSE

Oranges Are Not The Only Fruit, in both its manifestations, has taken people by surprise. As a book it came out quietly enough, rumbled as an underground success and then burst out winning the Whitbread prize for first novel. As a TV drama it began as an act of faith and proceeded without any fuss until its unveiling at the Film Festival. From that moment it has been a huge critical success and, just as important to me, a street success.

I know that *Oranges* challenges the virtues of the home, the power of the church and the supposed normality of hetero-sexuality. I was always clear that it would do. I would rather not have embarked on the project than see it toned down in any way. That all this should be the case and that it should still have been so overwhelmingly well received cheers me up. Perhaps TV, because it needs to entertain and be acceptable in a way that cinema does not, can still shock in the most profitable sense of the word. Perhaps TV can have a moral as well as a social function. Perhaps it can help us to question what morality really means.

The evangelical church, notably the Pentecostal branch, has been on the defensive – no bad thing for such a smug and self-righteous outfit. They have complained in their droves to the BBC, demanded air time and newspaper space and had their members telephone me day and night to explain the hellish penalty awaiting my damned soul. There is an odd contradiction between their readiness to identify themselves with the church scenes in *Oranges* and their vehement assertions that they are nothing like that. We never gave a name to our sect – we simply waited for it to be claimed.

Of course it's true that I was brought up by Pentecostals but I have drawn on a wide number of influences and experiences in creating my story. And it is my story, not my life, in spite of the deafening cries of 'autobiography' and questions such as, 'Were you tied up and gagged?'

Why do we try and pin things down all the time? Why do we cling to the 'real' over the imagined? Why do we attach more significance to what happened rather than to what might have happened?

When I was writing my scripts I was conscious of pushing the story further and further away from any discernable shoreline. Beeban and her cast set it adrift completely. Yes, an outline can still be found that resembles the past, but my mother should not recognise herself. Characters who never existed, never could exist, jostle alongside some that did. I don't know how much people believe of all this. What I do know is that it is the fusion of fact and fiction, the conscious and deliberate merging of different realities and unrealities, that makes *Oranges* so compelling. We claim we like to know what's what, to know how to separate story-telling, which is not fact, from history, which is fact. To know which is St George and which is the dragon. But another part of us longs to be taken somewhere where the rules are overturned and the signposts blurred. Somewhere just on the edge, so that we can get away if we want to, but we don't want to.

Oranges Are Not The Only Fruit is one such place.

Jeanette Winterson
London, 1990

ORANGES ARE NOT THE
ONLY FRUIT

Oranges Are Not The Only Fruit was first transmitted on BBC TV in January 1990, in three episodes.

The cast included:

MOTHER	Geraldine McEwan
JESS	Charlotte Coleman
ELSIE	Margery Withers
PASTOR FINCH	Kenneth Cranham
WILLIAM	Peter Gordon
MISS JEWSBURY	Celia Imrie
MELANIE	Cathryn Bradshaw
MAY	Elizabeth Spriggs
MRS GREEN	Freda Dowie
CISSY	Barbara Hicks
MRS ARKWRIGHT	Pam Ferris
SMALL JESS	Emily Aston
KATY	Tania Rodrigues

Director	Beeban Kidron
Producer	Phillippa Giles
Designer	Cecilia Brereton
Costume Designer	Les Lansdown

ONE

EXT. FAIRGROUND. FANTASY. NIGHT

An old-fashioned fairground with a merry-go-round and dodgems, a ghost-train and a tunnel of love. One-armed bandits, etc. but no modern games machines. Candy floss stalls, a strong man, a fortune teller's tent.

It's night-time, everything is lit up.

JESS *and* SMALL JESS *are walking hand in hand through the fairground. A barrel organ is churning out 'John Brown's Body'. The two of them look at it all in wonder and now and again smile at each other. As they go past the merry-go-round, they see Jess's* MOTHER *and* FATHER, MRS GREEN, MISS JEWSBURY *and* CISSY, PASTOR FINCH, MAY, MRS ARKWRIGHT, ELSIE, *and* MRS VIRTUE *riding the horses and waving and smiling.* JESS *and* SMALL JESS *wave back, looking from the teeth of the horses, with their wide lips and flared nostrils, to the wide smiles of the people riding them. They turn away and walk towards the tunnel of love.*

A carriage comes out with a figure [MELANIE] *seated inside wearing a cloak and hood and holding a mask to its face.* JESS *lets go of* SMALL JESS's *hand and gets into the carriage which disappears into the tunnel.* SMALL JESS *wanders over to the fortune teller's tent where the* OLD WOMAN *grabs her palm, scrutinises it and starts to laugh.*

OLD WOMAN: You'll never marry and you'll never be still.

[SMALL JESS *tries to pull away but the* WOMAN *holds on tight, laughing more and more wildly.* SMALL JESS *looks for help, but sees only the manic, whirling figures on the horses.*]

INT. SWEETSHOP. DAY

SMALL JESS, *out of breath, throws open the door of an old-*

fashioned sweetshop full of jars. Behind a counter stacked with papers are two cheerful women in their forties. They smile at SMALL JESS *as she comes in.*

SMALL JESS: It's me.

[*One of the women reaches under the counter and pulls out a pile of slightly ragged comics tied with hairy string. The other gives her a banana bar.* SMALL JESS *grabs the loot and rushes out.*]

EXT. STREET. DAY

SMALL JESS *runs home and arrives at her house. She lets herself in. Over shots of her running home the following is heard:*

JESS: [*As narrator*] Like most people, I lived for a long time with my mother and father. My father liked to watch the wrestling. My mother liked to wrestle. It didn't matter what. She was in the White Corner and that was that. She hung out the largest sheets on the windiest days. She wanted the Mormons to knock on her door.

[*Dialogue continues over next scene.*]

JESS: At election time in a Labour mill-town, my mother put a picture of the Conservative candidate in the window. She had never heard of mixed feelings; there were friends and there were enemies . . .

INT. HALL/KITCHEN. DAY

SMALL JESS *listens fleetingly at the parlour door, which is closed. She hears* MOTHER*'s voice shouting* 'Vengeance is mine saith the Lord'. *She shoves the comics under the mat at the bottom of the stairs, drops the banana bar down her jumper and shoots into the kitchen where the kettle is coming up to boil on the blazing blue jet of the stove. As it whistles, she brews the tea. The pot and mugs are already set out, a Bugs Bunny soft toy beside them. As soon as she has brewed the tea, she turns to face the door through which* MOTHER *will emerge. She stands to attention.*

A short pause and MOTHER *bursts through the door looking larger than life and radiant. She holds a huge copy of the Bible and advances towards the waiting* CHILD.

MOTHER: Who was the oldest man in the Bible?

SMALL JESS: Methusalah.

MOTHER: How old was he when he died?

SMALL JESS: Nine hundred and sixty nine.

MOTHER: What sort of tea is this?

   [*She looks in the pot.*]

SMALL JESS: Stand up and be counted . . .

   [*She salutes the towering figure, then looks muddled.*]
   I mean Empire Blend.

   [MOTHER *cuffs* JESS.]

INT. PARLOUR. DAY

MOTHER *and* SMALL JESS *sit either side of the radio.* MOTHER *picks up a pad and pencil from off the top of the set.*

MOTHER: Just in time for the Missionary Report.

SMALL JESS: Can I have my breakfast?

MOTHER: There'll be no breakfasts in Hell.

SMALL JESS: I'm not going to Hell.

MOTHER: No, not like all these Heathens in hot places we'll be hearing about when this set warms up.

INT. LIVING ROOM. DAY

MOTHER, SMALL JESS *and* WILLIAM *are sitting at table finishing their breakfast. Bugs Bunny is on a small chair next to* SMALL JESS. *A crooning ballad comes from the radiogram in the next room.*

MOTHER: I love to listen to the Jim Reeves Devotional Selection. What a singer!

   [WILLIAM *looks up from his plate and smiles.* MOTHER *stands up and adjusts herself.*]
   Come on Jess, we've got to take that dog for a walk, and then we'll come back and pray for all those Heathens in hot countries.

   [*She starts stacking the plates.* SMALL JESS *gets up and goes over to the dog in its basket.* WILLIAM *stays at the table eating the last bit of toast.*]

SMALL JESS: Are there more hot countries than cold ones?

MOTHER: I don't know. Fetch your hat and coat and put the dog on lead.

SMALL JESS: Not my hat.

MOTHER: Yes, your hat. Jesus is watching you.

EXT. STREET. DAY

MOTHER *takes* SMALL JESS's *hand.* SMALL JESS *has the dog on the lead in her other hand. They set off up the street towards the hill. As they pass next door, a* MAN *and a* WOMAN *push past them weighed down with cans of beer. They grin horribly at* MOTHER *and go inside. As they open their front door a wail of heavy metal music pours out.* MOTHER *hurries on.*

MOTHER: Drink, they spend all their money on drink and they're as filthy as anything. They've never seen soap or polish and they buy all their clothes from Maxi Ball's Catalogue Seconds. They can't afford new ones, they cut corners and swallow every penny. Don't you ever cut corners, Jess. I did it once myself, bought a cheap corset in the War, and a piece of the whalebone slipped right out the first time I wore it and stabbed me in the stomach all through Communion. There was nothing I could do but pray . . .

[*As* MOTHER *bangs on, they reach the sweetshop and* SMALL JESS *lags behind while* MOTHER *continues to talk.* SMALL JESS *taps on the window and waves.*]

MOTHER: [*cont.*] I still have that piece of whalebone, it's supporting the big geranium in the parlour.

[*She turns suddenly.*]

Are you listening, Jess? Come away from that shop, I've told you not to go there.

SMALL JESS: Why can't I? They give me old comics and they sell banana bars.

[MOTHER *grabs her hand and pulls her along.*]

MOTHER: I'm not going into it. All I'll say is that they deal in Unnatural Passions.

[*Pause.*]

SMALL JESS: Do you mean they put chemicals in their sweets?

MOTHER: Let it drop! I'll tell you a story. What about The Converted Sweep, a filthy drunken degenerate who had a vision one day while he was up in the flue of a big house. He stayed up there so long they thought he was dead, but when they got him down, his face, even covered in grime, shone like an angel's.

SMALL JESS: I've heard that one. Tell me another.

MOTHER: What about The Hallelujah Giant?

EXT. HILLTOP. DAY

Cut to top of the hill. The TWO of them are sitting down overlooking the town. The dog plays about.

SMALL JESS: I know that one.

MOTHER: He was more than eight feet high. Just imagine! One day he wandered into church and asked the faithful to pray for him. They did, they prayed mightily, and when he got measured at the clinic the following week, do you know what Jesus had done?

SMALL JESS: No . . .

[*It's clear she means yes.*]

MOTHER: I thought you knew this story . . .

[*She's pleased, even though she knows* SMALL JESS *is playing.*]

SMALL JESS: [*Gleeful*] What had Jesus done?

MOTHER: The good Lord had shrunk him to six foot three.

SMALL JESS: [*Dancing about*] Tell me another. Tell me about you.

MOTHER: I've told you that too!

[*She gets up and adjusts her coat and frock.*]

I used to be slim. When I first met the Lord I was as slim as anything. Of course, I'd been living in France.

SMALL JESS: What's French for dog?

MOTHER: I'm not teaching you French; you know it was nearly my downfall.

[MOTHER *adjusts her headscarf while* JESS *plays with the dog.*]

SMALL JESS: Did Pierre make you fall down?

MOTHER: Never you mind. Now listen to how I first met the Lord.

[*She takes* SMALL JESS *on her knee.*]

89

It was under canvas, down there, on that piece of spare land where they have the fair every year. Ellison's Tenement.

SMALL JESS: That's where I met the gypsy . . .

[*She holds out her palm but* MOTHER *ignores it.*]

MOTHER: There was a Glory Crusade going on and I heard the music and went in the tent. The preacher looked just like Errol Flynn but holy. [*She sighs.*] Yes, a lot of women found the Lord that week.

SMALL JESS: Was it our preacher?

MOTHER: No, it was Pastor Spratt and you know I still have his signed photo by my bed . . .

SMALL JESS: Next to the one of Pierre.

[MOTHER *glares then settles back.*]

MOTHER: He was on his way to hot places like Africa but he came to us and to Wigan first. When he said in his deep voice, 'Who wants to give their heart to Jesus?' I could hardly find my way to the front for tears. He gave me a copy of the Psalms and a pot plant. A lily of the valley it was. When your father went the next night I told him to try and get a cactus but by the time he'd got to the front they were all gone. He's not one to push himself. [*She pauses.*] Bless him . . .

[*She bends down and re-ties Jess's bonnet.*]

And after that we adopted you.

SMALL JESS: Too tight.

MOTHER: You'll be a missionary when you grow up.

SMALL JESS: Will I get a different hat?

MOTHER: [*Ignoring her*] This world is full of sin.

[*Close up on* MOTHER's *face as she says this. She stands up. A long shot of the hill and the town and the two of them standing side by side looking out and seeming quite alone and poignant.*]

MOTHER: You can change the world.

INT. JESS'S BEDROOM. DAY

MOTHER *walks into room, and wakes* SMALL JESS *up. She's got her hat and coat on. Bugs Bunny is curled up in* SMALL JESS's *arms.*

MOTHER: Jess.

SMALL JESS: What time is it?

MOTHER: Never mind, get up, we're going to Morecambe.

SMALL JESS: What for?

MOTHER: To do the Lord's work. There's others there from the church. I wasn't going to go what with your father working double shifts, but I've had a message [*points upwards*] and we're off. I've packed for you.

INT. KITCHEN. DAY

MOTHER *and* SMALL JESS *downstairs in hats and coats writing a note. We see a row of gleaming shoes by the sideboard and two suitcases, one large, one small. The note reads: 'Dear William, I am busy with the Lord in Morecambe.'*

EXT. MORECAMBE. DAY

A shot of the sea and the seagulls wheeling and dipping for food. Camera drops to reveal MOTHER *and* SMALL JESS *side by side on the prom.*

MOTHER: What a building! Morecambe Guest House for the Bereaved.

[*She takes* SMALL JESS*'s hand and they cross the road and go into the boarding house, resplendent with its sign saying:* The Morecambe Guest House for the Bereaved.]

INT. MORECAMBE GUEST HOUSE FOR THE BEREAVED. DAY

Inside there is a lobby with a room leading off, set with tables and tea things. CISSY *is sitting at one of the tables making wreaths. She glances up as* MOTHER *and* SMALL JESS *come in and come towards her. They sit at the same table.* SMALL JESS *props her Bugs Bunny on the fourth chair.*

MOTHER: I heard you'd be here. How many years is it?

CISSY: More than I want to count. Not since school. I've been living in Wales you know, doing wreaths freelance, but when I've finished this job here, I'm settling back on home ground near you.

MOTHER: Well I hope you'll come to church and find the Lord.

SMALL JESS: It's good at church.

CISSY: Who are you then? [*To* MOTHER.] Is she yours?

MOTHER: She is. This is Jess. Say hello to Cissy, Jess.

SMALL JESS: Hello.

CISSY: She's grand, isn't she? Here.

[*She offers* SMALL JESS *a sweet.* SMALL JESS *takes one.*]

MOTHER: You'd better not be sick again. [*To* CISSY.] It was vomit, vomit, vomit all the way here. I had to get off at Wigan and wash her down.

SMALL JESS: Can I go and play on the beach?

MOTHER: Don't you want to see everybody? The Reverend Eli Bone who runs the Society. Mrs Maude Butler from the Bereaved section?

SMALL JESS: No.

MOTHER: Who'd be a mother? Go on then, and watch out for the trams.

[SMALL JESS *shoots off,* MOTHER *sighs and plonks her bag on the table.*]

MOTHER: [*Bored*] Where is everybody?

CISSY: Your lot from the church are down on the beach. Reverend Bone'll be chasing from one corpse to another. He's been up all night with nothing between him and exhaustion but a flask of Typhoo. It's always the way, folk hang on through the winter, being stubborn, then spring comes, they relax, and *Bam!*

[*She thumps the table.*]

Flat out in no time. D'you fancy a brew of something hot?

MOTHER: No, I'll find the others.

[*She gets up.*]

CISSY: You set off and I'll get Jess and bring her along when she's ready. Kids like a bit of sand don't they?

MOTHER: Be careful with her.

EXT. MORECAMBE BEACH. DAY

MOTHER: [*Voice over*] She's my joy.

[SMALL JESS *squatting on the beach, building a sand castle.*

CISSY's *feet appear.* CISSY *bends down and gives* JESS *a handful of coloured flags.*]

CISSY: There, stick these in your castle.

SMALL JESS: Thank you. Do I have to go back?

CISSY: No. Let's have a stroll. You don't know me yet but I used to know your mother.

[*She takes* SMALL JESS's *hand and they walk along the seashore.*]

CISSY: What d'you think she'd like for a wreath? Something grand, eh?

SMALL JESS: You know the bit out of the Book of Revelation where everyone gets cast into the fiery pit? Can you do that?

CISSY: Well, it'll be a challenge. At least she don't fancy a cross. [CISSY *bends down and skims a pebble across the water. Camera on* SMALL JESS's *face watching it leap over the waves and disappear.*]

Are you the only one?

SMALL JESS: Yes.

CISSY: Your mum must love you.

SMALL JESS: She does. That's why she got me.

CISSY: You don't *get* children, you have them.

SMALL JESS: Somebody else had me, mum says it was a Bad Business, but after she got me it was all right again.

[CISSY *thoughtfully, half to herself.*]

CISSY: So you're not your mother's . . .

SMALL JESS: I am. I belong to her now, she filled in all the forms. She had to get a licence I think.

CISSY: That's for dogs.

SMALL JESS: We've got a dog, too. She's called Lassie.

CISSY: Well, maybe I'll come and see her when I come back up your way.

SMALL JESS: When?

CISSY: Soon enough. I'm going to make some money. When I get my own place, you'll see something then. People'll be lining the road to see my funerals go by. It'll be like the old days, a bit of respect and ceremony not chuck 'em in the oven with a bunch of lilies on top and go and have a meat sandwich after.

[*Cut to* ELSIE, MAY, MOTHER, MRS GREEN, MISS JEWSBURY *gathered on the sands. Two St John's Ambulance men are carrying an unknown woman away from them across the beach.*]

ELSIE: Think of the miracles of Jesus. You'll be up in no time.

MOTHER: What a terrible thing. It's Satan in our midst.

MRS GREEN: It's 'cos she was working for Jesus.

MAY: Who's going to play the castanets, then?

[SMALL JESS *comes rushing up panting. She leaps on* ELSIE.]

ELSIE: Oh no, I'm too old. You'll break my bones.

MOTHER: We should be praying, there's just been an accident.

SMALL JESS: Who's had an accident?

MOTHER: We were singing in the name of the Lord and Elsie was on the accordion and five young heathens came and laughed at us.

ELSIE: And one of them threw sand in my accordion and now I've no F Sharp. I'll have to use my decorating money to get it mended.

MISS JEWSBURY: We'll all help, Elsie.

ELSIE: Oh, thank you.

[MOTHER *clawing back the attention.*]

MOTHER: *And then*, Aunty Betty tried to chase them away and she fell and shouted that her leg had come loose.

MAY: I told her when she had her first one amputated that she should have her spare properly fitted, but she took no notice. She doesn't like hospitals.

ELSIE: Neither do I, men of knives, the lot of them. If they can cut it off or get it out they will. I knew a woman once . . .

MRS GREEN: Please, please, a word of prayer we said.

CISSY: [*Appearing*] What? No singing?

MAY: Oh, yes, let's have a chorus, let's have 'Cheer Up Ye Saints of God'. We need a bit of cheer now that Betty's gone.

SMALL JESS: Can I blow your oboe please, Miss Jewsbury?

MISS JEWSBURY: No, Jess, I'm fond of you but I don't want your spit today.

MAY: Come here, little 'un. Now look, I'm going to bang the drum and you can bang the tambourine. Because we both like to make a noise don't we?

[*As* SMALL JESS *goes over to her,* MAY *whispers.*]

Now look, don't mind Miss Jewsbury. Remember she's in an orchestra and she's Scottish.

[SMALL JESS *nods and takes the tambourine.* MOTHER *pushes her way to the front with a camera.*]

MOTHER: I'm going to take a photograph.

CISSY: Can I be in it?

MOTHER: It's supposed to be a photograph of the redeemed.

CISSY: Well, maybe it'll encourage me.

SMALL JESS: Let her be in it.

[*She takes* CISSY's *hand and leads her into the group. With her other hand she takes hold of* ELSIE. *The others shuffle up together.*]

MRS GREEN: Praise the Lord.

MOTHER: Everyone smile and think of the Second Coming.

[*She clicks. It freezes.*]

What a photo!

INT. BATHROOM. DAY

MOTHER *and* SMALL JESS *are in the bathroom.* MOTHER *is grouting the tiles. Plumbers' waste lies strewn about.* SMALL JESS *is holding an unopened letter and eating an orange.* MOTHER *doesn't notice. She's facing the other way and talking.*

MOTHER: We'll soon have this bathroom finished and once we've got a proper flushing toilet you won't have to use a bucket in the night. Your father'll be pleased. He doesn't say much but he notices.

SMALL JESS: Is he in bed now?

MOTHER: He's on nights this week, so you be quiet.

SMALL JESS: When you're in bed he gets up and when he gets up you're in bed.

[*She says this in a sing-song sort of way.*]

MOTHER: I don't want to talk about our habits, Jess.

[*She turns round and notices the letter.*]

What's that you've covered in orange dripping? [*She takes it.*] It must be a letter of thanks from The Society for the Lost for all our work in Morecambe.

[*She rips it open and looks at it. Her face clouds over.*]

95

SMALL JESS: What does it say?

MOTHER: It's from the Devil.

[SMALL JESS *is fascinated. She tries to see.*]

SMALL JESS: What does he want? What colour is the ink?

MOTHER: I mean, it's the Devil's work, they say if I don't send you to school right away they'll summons me before the courts.

SMALL JESS: Will you have to go to prison?

MOTHER: I don't know. Oh, it's a breeding ground. Let's have a word of prayer.

[MOTHER *pulls* SMALL JESS *down on to the floor and holds her hands up in prayer.*]

SMALL JESS: What's a breeding ground?

MOTHER: School.

SMALL JESS: But what is it?

MOTHER: It's like the sink would be if I didn't put bleach down it. Oh, what a trial.

SMALL JESS: I won't go.

MOTHER: And what would Next Door say if I was carted off to prison leaving you and father to manage by yourselves. Think how they'd jeer and mock.

SMALL JESS: St Paul was always going to prison.

MOTHER: I know that but the neighbours don't.

INT. KITCHEN/HALL. DAY

As SMALL JESS *comes into the kitchen.*

MOTHER: What hyacinths?

SMALL JESS: It said in the letter from the Devil that they're having a hyacinth growing competition at school. Elsie gave me some bulbs but you're supposed to put them in an airing cupboard and we haven't got one.

MOTHER: You don't need an airing cupboard when you've got Jesus.

[*There's a loud banging from the front door.*]

What a din, it's like Judgement Day. You get your bulbs out and I'll have a look when I've been to the door. It'll be that window cleaner I bet.

[*Focus on* SMALL JESS *getting out her bulbs from behind the*

*Bugs Bunny who's sitting on one of the kitchen units by a huge
bowl of oranges.*
  Suddenly SMALL JESS *and we hear a commotion at the door.*
SMALL JESS, *bulb in hand, creeps down the lobby and sees and
hears the following scene.*
  MOTHER *is standing on the doorstep, arms outstretched across
the doorway like the crucified Christ. On the pavement is a
much younger pretty* WOMAN, *not well-dressed but clean and
obviously upset.*]

MOTHER: I told you never to come here again. I told you, didn't I?

WOMAN: You don't have to tell her who I am. Tell her what you
like, just let me see her.

MOTHER: You'll never see her. You gave her away. You were glad
enough then, weren't you, running off with your fancy man?

WOMAN: I was seventeen. She's still my daughter.

MOTHER: She's not your daughter. She's mine. You were unfit –
unfit to have a child.

WOMAN: Just let me see her.

MOTHER: God gave her to me.

WOMAN: You've nothing to do with God. You've a heart of stone.
  [*The* WOMAN *lunges forward and tries to push through.*
MOTHER *pushes her back and slaps her across the face.*]

MOTHER: You'll be in Hell.
  [*She slams the door and leans on it looking down the lobby. She
sees* SMALL JESS *thunderstruck by it all.*]
  Who told you to come out here?
  [SMALL JESS *says nothing.* MOTHER *goes and kneels before her
and shakes her shoulders.*]
  I said, who told you?

SMALL JESS: Was that my real mother?
  [MOTHER *pulls* SMALL JESS's *face very close. This must be
menacing.*]

MOTHER: I'm your real mother. She was just the carrying case that
bore you.
  [*She stands up and goes upstairs. We hear her slam the
bedroom door.*
SMALL JESS *goes to the front door and opens it quietly. The
street seems to be full of women. Which one is hers?*]

EXT. FRONT STEP. DAY

She sits down on the front step, the front door wide open, her knees drawn up. As she does this, a clarinet can be heard: 'Mine Eyes Have Seen the Glory of the Coming of the Lord' (3 lines) 'His Truth is Marching On' (1 line) then into the chorus of 'Glory Glory Hallelujah'. Softly, voices join in and carry across the scene change into the church.

INT. CHURCH. DAY

Camera cuts to the church service and a rousing chorus of 'Glory Glory', etc. Piano accompaniment; tambourines much in evidence. The church looks like the interior of a village hall. Ordinary chairs face a raised platform where the PASTOR *is standing. There is a piano on the right and a cross on the rear wall. Down one side of the church is a long table spread with sandwiches and trifles. Chairs are arranged around it. The* CONGREGATION *should be singing and clapping. As the chorus comes to an end there is a great flourish of tambourines and everyone, including* PASTOR, *starts clapping as though they are applauding someone. We can see* MOTHER *and* DAD, *the Morecambe gang and* SMALL JESS.]

PASTOR: Yes, yes, a big round of applause for Jesus. What a saviour! Hallelujah!

[*He holds up his hands to quiet everyone.*]

You've heard today in my sermon how the agencies of Satan try to tempt us, and I tell you, brothers and sisters, that the holier you are the more you will be tempted.

MOTHER: [*Shouting out*] Amen! Amen!

PASTOR: Some of you may meet the Unsaved who are so low in themselves and so high in the Devil's sight, that they are possessed by demons.

[*A shudder runs through the* CONGREGATION, *including cries of* 'No Jesus, heal their hearts!']

PASTOR: The signs of those possessed is that they will often burst into wild laughter, that they will engage in depraved sexual practices like St Paul warns us of in the first chapter of Romans, and that they are always very cunning. Indeed, brothers and sisters, Satan himself appeared as an angel of light! Ponder these things in your heart while we eat our sandwiches together, sharing our food like the disciples of old. Then, as now, the demon would get in where he could and the Devil is still ruler of this world. I see your hand, sister, what is it?

[ELSIE NORRIS *struggles to her feet.*]

ELSIE: I just want you all to know what when I came into church today I had terrible wind but now the Lord has taken it away.

PASTOR: Praise the Lord. Bless you, Elsie for testifying. The Lord gave you that wind so that he could take it away. Amen, Amen. Now don't forget to pick up your free copies of *The Plain Truth*.

[*The piano starts up on the chorus again and everyone joins in as they make their way over to the table laden with food.* PASTOR *waves one hand above his head and goes towards the table.*]

ELSIE: [*To* MOTHER.] It's Elijah in our midst again.

MOTHER: It is, it is. Let me help you sit down.

ELSIE: Oh I'm all right, thank you dear.

MOTHER: That was a lovely sermon you gave today, Pastor Finch. It's not fashionable to talk about the Devil and his demons, but we have to know don't we?

PASTOR FINCH: We do. These are the last days when many will find themselves possessed by the Devil. Did you make these sandwiches?

MOTHER: [*Coy*] And the sherry trifle.

PASTOR FINCH: You can tell a good woman by her sandwiches.

[SMALL JESS *reaches out to grab another sandwich but* PASTOR *grabs her wrist. He's far too heavy-handed for the situation. The people around the table fall silent.*]

How old are you now, Jessica?

SMALL JESS: Seven.

PASTOR FINCH: Seven. How blessed. The seven days of creation, the seven-branched candlestick. The seven seals . . .

SMALL JESS: [*Fidgeting and hungry*] What did they eat?

PASTOR FINCH: Who?

SMALL JESS: The seven seals.

PASTOR: Nothing. [*He's confused.*]

ELSIE: [*Leaning across*] He's not talking about things with fins — he means seal like in sealing wax.

PASTOR: Yes, that's right. You should read the Book of Revelation. Seven. How blessed. But how *cursed*!

[*Everyone has gone quiet.*]

The demon can return seven-fold! This little lily,

[*He seizes* SMALL JESS's *hand again, sandwich included.*]

this bloom of the covenant, could herself become a house of demons.

ELSIE: Steady on, Pastor.

[*He ignores her.*]

PASTOR: I've known the most holy of men suddenly become filled with evil. How much more a woman! And how much more a child! Husbands, watch your wives. Parents, watch your children. Blessed be the word of the Lord.

MOTHER: Amen, Pastor, Amen.

[PASTOR *lets go of* SMALL JESS *who climbs down from the table and goes into a small side room.*]

ELSIE: I think you were a bit strong there, Pastor.

PASTOR: I was firm, Elsie, firm.

ELSIE: I'll go and see if she's all right.

PASTOR: No, no, I'll go.

[ELSIE *shakes her head as* PASTOR *heads for the little room.* SMALL JESS *is sitting on the floor. She's making a picture.*]

PASTOR: [*Crouching down*] What's that?

SMALL JESS: Daniel in the Lions' Den.

PASTOR: But that's not right! In your picture the lions are swallowing Daniel. But, he was saved by the Lord.

SMALL JESS: Well, I got a bit mixed up. I wanted to do Jonah and the Whale. He got swallowed, but you don't do whales in fuzzy felt.

PASTOR: Let's put it right, shall we? We'll just take Daniel out of the Lion's mouth and we'll have him saying good morning to the Heathen King Nebuchadnezzar.

SMALL JESS: There aren't any kings left. Susan Green was sick over the tableau of the Three Wise Men and you only get three to a box.

[PASTOR *isn't listening. He's rooting through the fuzzy felt and muttering happily.* SMALL JESS *wanders off, only to be collared by* MISS JEWSBURY *clutching her oboe.*]

MISS JEWSBURY: Where's the Pastor?

SMALL JESS: He's in the Sunday School room playing with the fuzzy felt.

MISS JEWSBURY: Don't be fanciful Jessica.

[*Before* SMALL JESS *can argue,* MOTHER *appears and starts putting* SMALL JESS *into her coat and bonnet.* MISS JEWSBURY *turns away.* MRS GREEN *appears looking pious.*]

MRS GREEN: She's not holy, that Miss Jewsbury.

MOTHER: She's not, Mrs Green. Not married either and well past thirty.

SMALL JESS: Pastor's not married and he's past thirty.

MOTHER: Will you stop it? Someone might hear you.

SMALL JESS: It's true. Anyway she's going to give me lessons on her oboe.

MOTHER: She's not.

SMALL JESS: She said so.

MOTHER: She is not. I'll speak to her about that.

[MOTHER *prepares to confront* MISS JEWSBURY *who's standing near by chatting to* ELSIE. MRS GREEN *lays a restraining hand on* MOTHER.]

SMALL JESS: Can we go home now? I'm starting school in the morning Mrs Green and they're giving me a test to see what I know.

MOTHER: It's how you live your life that's the test. Come on.

[MOTHER *pats* MRS GREEN's *arm and stops glaring at* MISS JEWSBURY.]

EXT. STREET. DAY

Out on the street.

MOTHER *and* MRS GREEN *lead the procession, followed by* WILLIAM *and* MAY *then* SMALL JESS *and* ELSIE *holding hands.*

ELSIE: I never thought your mother would send you to school. She wanted to do it all herself.

SMALL JESS: She's got to, otherwise they're going to send her to prison.

ELSIE: That's not bad. I've been in prison.

SMALL JESS: What for?

ELSIE: Votes for Women. It was a long time ago.

SMALL JESS: Mum doesn't want to go to prison; she wants to look after me and Dad.

ELSIE: I'm getting my accordion back this week. You can come and play on it for a treat after school.

SMALL JESS: And the organ. I'll push the pedals so that you don't get out of breath and wheeze.

ELSIE: Are you looking forward to school?

SMALL JESS: Yes, but mum says it's a breeding ground.

(ELSIE *laughs;* SMALL JESS *continues.*]

What about my hyacinths? Will Jesus make them grow without an airing cupboard?

ELSIE: He will if you ask him. Whenever I ask him he always does it. Last week I had no eggs and I asked Jesus about it and what do you think?

SMALL JESS: What?

ELSIE: When I looked out in the back yard one of them hens from the allotments had flown over and was laying right beneath the laburnum tree. Praise the Lord.

SMALL JESS: Will you ask him about the hyacinths then?

ELSIE: I will. Look out this is my turning. Goodnight, Jess. Now you get a good night's sleep and be bright as a button tomorrow.

[*She bends down and kisses her as they catch up with the other four waiting at the corner.*]

MOTHER: Mrs Norris, William will walk down with you. We'll go on, if you don't mind.

ELSIE: Oh, I'll be safe with William.

[*She takes his proffered arm.*]

Goodnight all. God bless.

[*The others chorus* 'Goodnight, God bless' *and set off.* MAY *takes* SMALL JESS's *hand.* MOTHER *and* MRS GREEN *continue.*]

SMALL JESS: Got any sweets, May?

MAY: No, I ate 'em all.

SMALL JESS: So did I.

[*There is a terrific thunderclap. They look up at the black sky in dismay as the rain comes pouring down. Suddenly a door opens off the street and a* WOMAN's *raucous voice yells out.*]

MRS ARKWRIGHT: May! Come in here out of the rain.

MAY: Ooh, it's Nettie Arkwright, we're in luck. Come on Jess before you catch your death of cold.

[*They disappear into the shop.*]

MOTHER: I can't go in that shop.

MRS GREEN: Perhaps we're meant as a testimony. Jesus himself associated with tax-collectors and sinners, besides, it's pouring down.

[*They huddle in the adjacent doorway.*]

She's a terrible Heathen.

MOTHER: I know. Let's not say it on a Sunday.

[MRS ARKWRIGHT *re-appears.*]

MRS ARKWRIGHT: Get in here out of the rain. You'll die of cold.

MOTHER: At least I know where I'm going.

[MRS ARKWRIGHT *screeches with laughter saying* 'Oh, aye, very good that, yes . . .' *and shoos* MOTHER *and* MRS GREEN *in through the door. As* MOTHER *and* MRS GREEN *disappear inside Mrs Arkwright's, we see the sign above the shop:* 'Arkwright's for Vermin'.]

INT. ARKWRIGHT'S. DAY

Inside, the shop is Dickensian in its squalor. There is a rough counter, stacks of boxes and sacks of oddments. Four chairs are drawn up around a paraffin stove. MRS ARKWRIGHT *remains standing throughout. Before sitting down,* MOTHER *dusts her chair with a hanky.* SMALL JESS *and* MAY *seem quite happy.*

MRS ARKWRIGHT: Swig o' tea anybody?

[*She picks up a huge mug and offers it around.*]

Where've you been, May? I've not seen hide of you in a month.

MAY: I've been at Blackpool, resting. I've come into some money. Bingo. Housie Housie three times.

MRS GREEN: I thought you'd stopped your gambling ways.

SMALL JESS: Have you got any 'Snap' cards, May?

MOTHER: Auntie May to you and no 'Snap'.

MAY: I've come to an arrangement with the Lord. If I win I'm giving him ten per cent.

MRS ARKWRIGHT: Happen I'll try that, I could do with some luck.

MRS GREEN: It's holiness you need, Mrs Arkwright, not luck.

MOTHER: Amen! I'll leave you a copy of *The Plain Truth*.

MRS ARKWRIGHT: Well, there's no money in vermin anymore.

MAY: No, folk are cleaner than they were.

MRS ARKWRIGHT: I'm hoping we'll have a hot summer. That'll fetch 'em out.

MRS GREEN: What do you mean, Mrs Arkwright?

MRS ARKWRIGHT: Remember that heatwave we had two years back? Ooh, I did some trade then. What days they were. Hardbacks, cockroaches, rats, lice, you name it, I poisoned it.

[MOTHER *starts blowing her nose and coughing*.]

MAY: I remember, you got your name in the paper.

MRS ARKWRIGHT: That's right. 'A Service to Industry' they called me. Because I got rid of them beetles the Mayor found in his robes. Well, you can't be a public figure and full o' bugs.

MAY: Oh, you can't. People lose confidence.

MOTHER: I think it's stopped raining.

MRS ARKWRIGHT: No hurry, it's still spitting. Stop and have a drop of supper. I've got kidney and sausages.

[*She pulls out a string of sausages and holds them up*.]

MAY: Lovely. I'll stay.

SMALL JESS: So will I.

[MRS GREEN *looks like she's going to be sick*.]

MOTHER: We can't stay. Jess starts school tomorrow – it's her first day and she's got a test. Come on May, Mrs Green.

MAY: Nay, I'll stop a bit.

MRS ARKWRIGHT: Take these tins of flea powder. I don't like to see you go empty-handed. There. Go on. Bye bye, Mrs Green. Bye.

[MRS ARKWRIGHT *shoves the tins at* MOTHER *and ushers her and* MRS GREEN *out of the door, shouting her goodbyes*.]

INT. LIVING ROOM. DAY

MOTHER *with her back to us throwing shovel-fulls of coal onto an already blazing fire. She does this in rhythm with her first words.*

MOTHER: Shadrach, [*shovel of coal*] Mesach [*shovel of coal*] and Abednego [*shovel of coal*] in the fiery furnace.

[*The camera pulls back further to reveal* SMALL JESS *in her socks, knickers and vest standing to one side of the fire, eating a piece of toast. Warming on a chair next to her is a duffle coat. On top of it, a Collins English Gem dictionary.*]

SMALL JESS: I know! The wicked king Nebuchadnezzar wanted them to burn to death, but an angel got in the furnace too and they were saved.

[MOTHER *stands up and pulls a gym-slip out from under the coat. The dictionary falls to the floor;* SMALL JESS *retrieves it.*]

MOTHER: It's going to be like that at school. Now, put this on.

SMALL JESS: Why is school like the fiery furnace?

MOTHER: It's a trial, that's why.

[*She starts putting* SMALL JESS *into the gym-slip.*]

SMALL JESS: It's back to front.

[MOTHER *whips it round the right way.*]

MOTHER: Oh, I can't concentrate, I haven't been to bed all night.

SMALL JESS: Why not?

MOTHER: No point if I had to get up with you so early. By the time I'd ironed your gym-slip and prayed for everybody and soaked my feet and made your Dad's sandwiches, I thought, I might as well sit and read the Bible and wait for you. Life's a sacrifice.

SMALL JESS: Where's Dad?

MOTHER: Gone to work. I saw him off at 5 o'clock like I always do when he's on earlies.

SMALL JESS: And then you go to bed.

[MOTHER *hands* SMALL JESS *her shoes.*]

MOTHER: Yes, now, put these on and tie them tight. But now that you've started school I won't be able to go to bed at all. I'll have to take a nap on the settee.

SMALL JESS: Will you keep your clothes on?

MOTHER: Save your questions for school. Now put your duffle coat on.

[*She holds out the duffle coat,* SMALL JESS *struggles into it.*]

SMALL JESS: I'm excited.

MOTHER: I don't know why, it's not like going to church. Now, you know your tables and you can read and write and do sums.

SMALL JESS: Adding and take away.

MOTHER: And you've got your pocket Bible for when you feel oppressed.

SMALL JESS: And I've got my dictionary from Elsie.

MOTHER: And when it's play-time go and pray. I'll be praying for you all day.

SMALL JESS: Elsie's praying, too. She's asking Jesus about my bulbs.

[MOTHER *kneels down and kisses* SMALL JESS *and holds her hands.*]

MOTHER: Just remember when you're out in the world and all its sin that you belong to the Lord and you belong to me.

[SMALL JESS *nods gravely.*]

EXT. PLAYING FIELDS. DAY

CHILDREN *playing.* SMALL JESS *sitting, watching.*

INT. CLASSROOM. DAY

A bell is ringing violently, children playing around in a classroom rush to their desks and try and look orderly. Most children share a desk. SMALL JESS *is alone at the front looking anxious.* MRS VIRTUE *arrives and the class sits down.*

MRS VIRTUE: Now, we've all got to know our new girl, Jessica, this morning and she's been writing us a little story about what she did before she started school. I think you've finished it now, haven't you?

SMALL JESS: Yes, Mrs Virtue.

MRS VIRTUE: Then don't be shy. It's very good that you can read and write already.

SMALL JESS: [*Reads the title*] 'My Trip To Morecambe With Our Church Camp.'

[MRS VIRTUE *nods encouragement and smiles.*]

SMALL JESS: My mother is Treasurer of The Society for The Lost in Morecambe. Its Headquarters are at The Morecambe Guest House for the Bereaved where you can go when you're upset. [MRS VIRTUE *begins to look a bit worried, but the class are perking up.*]

We go and stay there and preach the gospel on the beach, but this time Auntie Betty's leg came loose and my mother struggled mightily to hold her up.

MRS VIRTUE: Is your mother a nurse, Jessica?

SMALL JESS: No, but she heals the sick.

[*Sniggers from the class.* MRS VIRTUE *glares and hushes them.*]

MRS VIRTUE: Well, carry on then.

SMALL JESS: Before that some heathens came and threw sand in Elsie Norris's accordion and now she's no F sharp.

One of the children farts, SMALL JESS *pauses and continues.*]

When we got back, Next Door had had another baby but there are so many of them next door we don't know who's it is. Mother said they breed like rabbits. We gave them some carrots but they threw them back over the wall and shouted that they weren't a charity.

[*The class have gone very quiet.* SMALL JESS *looks up at* MRS VIRTUE.]

MRS VIRTUE: Is there anymore?

SMALL JESS: Yes, two more sides.

MRS VIRTUE: What about?

SMALL JESS: Not much, just how we hired the baths for our baptism service after the healing of the sick crusade.

MRS VIRTUE: Very good, but I don't think we have time today. We must talk about our samplers now. I'll show you what I want you to do.

[SMALL JESS *sits down slowly amongst giggles from the class.* MRS VIRTUE *holds up a nicely embroidered sampler.*]

Now, I'm going to teach you all to do chain stitch, cross stitch and hem stitch. Not at once but bit by bit and everyone can make their own sampler like this one. You must each think of a few words to embroider onto it, and we'll give you a prize for the best one. For instance, you might want to embroider, 'I love Mummy'.

[SMALL JESS *is seen waving her hand.*]
Yes, Jessica?
SMALL JESS: Does it have to be for mothers?
MRS VIRTUE: No, Jess. Please don't feel you have to make it for your mother.
[*She's clearly nervous.*]
SMALL JESS: Well, I'll make it for my friend then.
MRS VIRTUE: Lovely. Is that a friend in our class?
SMALL JESS: No. It's for Elsie Norris. She's old and her teeth don't fit, but she likes reading the Bible.
MRS VIRTUE: Well then, why not embroider 'God is love'?
SMALL JESS: I was thinking I'd do 'The summer is ended and we are not yet saved'.
[*Shot of* MRS VIRTUE's *face.*]

INT. HEADMISTRESS' STUDY/CORRIDOR. DAY.

MRS VIRTUE *and* MRS VOLE *are walking along corridor.*
MRS VIRTUE: I've written to her mother but it will do no good. Yesterday I had Mrs Spencer and Mrs Sparrow in my classroom; their daughters were in tears with the torments Jessica had devised. She told Yvonne she'd never be able to use a proper toilet in hell, and Julie that she'd spend all her time talking to people who couldn't hear her.
MRS VOLE: That's rather sophisticated, isn't it? Didn't she mention boiling oil?
MRS VIRTUE: You're not taking me seriously. Her mother doesn't want her at school, she wants to train her to be a missionary.
MRS VOLE: Well, bring her in, I'll talk to her.
[*They arrive at Mrs Vole's office.* SMALL JESS *is crouched outside talking to herself.*]
MRS VIRTUE: Come in, Jessica.

INT. PARLOUR. NIGHT

SMALL JESS *is sitting in front of the fire making something out of paper. She looks feverish. On the floor beside her in its frame is the sampler.* MOTHER *is sitting on the settee looking through some sheet music.*

MOTHER: I like that sampler. Can I have it?

SMALL JESS: No, it's for Elsie. I want it to win a prize, but I don't think it will.

MOTHER: Don't fill your mind with thoughts of prizes. Years ago, when I had my figure, we used to have a competition for the face that most inspired young men to think of Jesus. I won it for five years running. And the year I didn't win, I thought that's it, my figure's gone. But soon after I realised it was the Lord gently pushing me to be even more spiritual. So bear that in mind.

SMALL JESS: [*Nodding gravely*] I won't mind then. [*She pauses and wipes her brow.*] I'm hot and my eyes hurt.

MOTHER: Well come away from that fire then and stop staring at that bit of paper you've got.

[SMALL JESS *moves and sits next to* MOTHER.]

SMALL JESS: Can I get a drink of water?

MOTHER: I'll get your supper in a minute. You can have custard.

SMALL JESS: I've got to make friends with the other children.

MOTHER: I won't have you associating with the limbs of Satan. We're called to be apart.

SMALL JESS: I am apart, but I like Eileen. She walked home with me today when I wasn't feeling very well.

MOTHER: I'm not surprised. How can you feel well spending all day in a Den of Vice.

SMALL JESS: Can Eileen come and see me next week after school?

MOTHER: Is she saved?

SMALL JESS: No but she's nice.

MOTHER: Invite her to church.

SMALL JESS: She's a Catholic.

MOTHER: They're the worst. I won't have you misled by the smooth tongues of priests.

SMALL JESS: I never see any priests.

MOTHER: A girl's motto is, 'Be prepared'.

SMALL JESS: I can't hear you very well.

MOTHER: What's the matter?

SMALL JESS: I don't know.

MOTHER: [*Shouting*] It'll be the Lord blocking your ears to all but the words of the Spirit.

SMALL JESS: I heard you then.

MOTHER: That's because I'm telling the truth. It's a miracle, a miracle in our midst. Wait till I tell the Pastor.

[*She comes up very close to* SMALL JESS *and puts her hands on each side of her cheeks.*]

INT. CHURCH. DAY

PASTOR, MAY, MRS GREEN *and* MOTHER *are grouped round a chair where* SMALL JESS *is sitting facing the* CONGREGATION. *She looks ill.*

PASTOR: A miracle in our midst.

MOTHER: Amen. Amen.

PASTOR: Our own Jess has been so blessed by the Lord that she can't hear a word we're saying. She's abandoned the things of this world for the things of the spirit. Her own mother and these good women have told me how she's neither heard nor spoken for a week now. These are the signs and wonders promised for the last day before Jesus returns.

MRS GREEN: It's holiness. True holiness.

PASTOR: And now we're going to sing a chorus, and while we sing it, I want anyone who has a problem to come to the front and touch Jess and leave their burden with her. No harm can come to her; she's protected by Angels. Mrs Green, would you play for us please?

[MRS GREEN *goes over to the piano and strikes up the chorus.* MAY *gets out her tambourine,* MOTHER *and* PASTOR *clap.* SMALL JESS *sits oblivious, looking sick. The singing is wild and frenetic.*

Various members of the congregation come forward and touch SMALL JESS *and return to their seats while* PASTOR *nods and smiles.*

MISS JEWSBURY *comes forward and puts a hand to* SMALL JESS's *forehead, then to her throat. She starts to take her pulse but* PASTOR *tries to motion her away. She stands up and starts talking to* MOTHER.]

MISS JEWSBURY: Jess, Jess! Will you listen to me? Your daughter's ill. She has a fever and swollen glands.

[*As she talks, the stream of people continues to come up and down but we can hear* MISS JEWSBURY *clearly above the music.*]

PASTOR: It's the age of miracles, Miss Jewsbury. Perhaps you'd be better off as a Methodist.

MISS JEWSBURY: I'm telling you she's ill and she has to have a doctor.

MAY: Don't doubt the power of the Lord. I did and I was proved wrong.

MOTHER: I know my own child, Miss Jewsbury.

PASTOR: Amen, Amen. You should look to your faith.

MISS JEWSBURY: There's nothing wrong with my faith.

[*As she says this,* SMALL JESS *slumps off the chair in a dead faint.*]

INT. HOSPITAL WARD. DAY

SMALL JESS *is lying in a hospital bed. She opens her eyes and sees a* DOCTOR *and* NURSE *standing by her. Both are in white.*

SMALL JESS: Am I in Heaven?

DOCTOR: No, but this is an Angel.

[*The* NURSE *blushes.*]

We had to take out your adenoids and your tonsils. You couldn't hear a thing, all clogged up like that. Now, you've had an anaesthetic so you'll be feeling a bit groggy. Nurse will look after you.

[*He strokes her hand.*]

Oh, you've a visitor, Jess. We'll be on our way. Come on, Angel.

(MOTHER *arrives with a bulging bag of oranges. As* MOTHER *talks she starts piling them into the hospital bowl and then, when she runs out of room, she fills up the top of the locker with them.*]

MOTHER: Hello Jess. I've brought you some fruit and a copy of *The Plain Truth*. Why didn't you tell me you were ill?

SMALL JESS: I didn't know I was ill.

MOTHER: Well, I'm sure Jesus had his reasons. It was my prayers that pulled you through. More people die under anaesthetic than they do water-skiing. Terrible. That's why I don't believe in doctors.

SMALL JESS: Will you bring my Bugs Bunny?

MOTHER: Next time. I've got to go now. We've got a prayer meeting on. I just wanted you to know that I'm here.

[*She stands up to go.*

ELSIE *comes up to the bed and plonks down a box.*]

ELSIE: Hello both. I've brought a present.

MOTHER: I have to be off. Say prayers with her for me. Goodbye, Elsie. Goodbye, Jess.

[*She rolls away.*]

ELSIE: Where's she off to in such a rush?

SMALL JESS: The prayer meeting. Aren't you going?

ELSIE: No. I'm visiting you. Miss Jewsbury asked me to give you this and then you can have what I've fetched.

[*She hands* SMALL JESS *a book. It's a picture edition of 'Beauty and the Beast'.*]

SMALL JESS: Beauty and the Beast.

ELSIE: That's right. A princess marries a horrible beast but it's all right in the end. You won't be frightened.

SMALL JESS: [*Flicking through it*] Like May. She married a pig. She said he was a real pig too.

ELSIE: She didn't mean it.

SMALL JESS: She did. I asked her twice. I'll lend her this book when I've read it.

ELSIE: Are you all right?

SMALL JESS: I thought I'd died because the doctor told me the nurse was an Angel and patted her a lot. But you don't pat Angels do you?

INT. SCHOOL HALL. DAY

A school hall with a long table laid out with lots of hyacinths in pots. Some have prize numbers on them or special commendations. SMALL JESS *in her coat and hat is standing in front of the table looking at the hyacinths. She seems puzzled. A teacher,* MRS VIRTUE, *comes up and starts fiddling around.*

MRS VIRTUE: Hello Jess. You're still a bit pale after your illness aren't you? You should be on your way home. Everyone's gone.

SMALL JESS: I wanted to see if I'd won a prize.

MRS VIRTUE: We can't all win prizes.

SMALL JESS: Did you like mine?

MRS VIRTUE: Which one was yours?

[SMALL JESS *goes to the end of the table and points out a couple of pink blooms leaning together.*]

SMALL JESS: I grew them for Jesus. They're called 'The Annunciation'. They're Mary and Elizabeth just after the Angel had been to tell them the good news.

MRS VIRTUE: Very nice.

SMALL JESS: Why did 'Snow Sisters' win and not mine?

[*Camera focuses on a pair of white hyacinths in a posh pot.*]

MRS VIRTUE: Winning doesn't matter.

SMALL JESS: Why do you give prizes then?

MRS VIRTUE: I think you should go home now. Go on.

SMALL JESS: Things take a long time to grow don't they? We haven't got an airing cupboard at home. I grew them in a bin bag under the gas oven.

[MRS VIRTUE *looks at her and walks away.*

SMALL JESS *stares at 'Snow Sisters' then at her own blooms. She picks up the hyacinths and walks off down the long deserted hall.*]

INT. LIVING ROOM. DAY

MOTHER, ELSIE, MAY, MRS GREEN *and* SMALL JESS *are in the living room of mother's house, taking off their hats and coats. They're clearly in their Sunday best.*

MOTHER: What a sermon! What a speaker!

MAY: You can't beat the Lord's day. I love a Sunday.

MRS GREEN: Oh it was holy today, though I noticed that Miss Jewsbury nodded off in communion again.

[MOTHER *and* MRS GREEN *tut and shake their heads.*]

MAY: Well, I've been known to nod off myself.

[MOTHER *and* MRS GREEN *glare at her.* ELSIE *is helping* SMALL JESS *with her coat.*]

MOTHER: Come on Jess, you can do it yourself. I want you to lay the table while I get the cabbage on. No cabbage, no dinner.

[MRS GREEN *laughs*.]

MRS GREEN: The Lord will help it simmer. I'll give you a hand in the kitchen.

MOTHER: We'll have to be quiet because William's working nights this week and he hasn't been home off his overtime shift long. So if the spirit moves any of you to cry out, try not to do it in the direction of the back bedroom. Sit down all, sit down.

[*They start arranging themselves*.]

ELSIE: Can I trouble you for your toilet?

MOTHER: You can. It's still outside.

ELSIE: [*Departing*] Best place for it. You don't want all that muck inside.

[*Suddenly noises are heard coming through the wall from next door. Clearly somebody is fucking, although* SMALL JESS *doesn't recognise it as such. Everybody freezes for a second.* MRS GREEN *crushes her ear to the wall.*]

SMALL JESS: Is somebody ill?

MRS GREEN: Whatever it is, it's not holy.

[*She turns to* MOTHER *who is horrified.* MOTHER *goes to a huge cupboard and opens it. It's stacked with tins of food.*]

MOTHER: This is my War Cupboard for when the holocaust comes. Every home should have one.

[*She routs behind some tins, flinging a pile at* SMALL JESS *who tries to hold them.*]

I might have something behind these special offer sardines.

MAY: Oh, I hope they're in tomato sauce. Brine's bad for you.

[MOTHER *reaches out a box of glasses and gives one to* MRS GREEN. MAY *takes another and the two of them start slithering up and down the wall, listening through the glasses.*]

MOTHER: We've just had that wall decorated.

MAY: They've stopped anyhow.

[*As they stand straight up, looking relieved, another blast comes through the wall. Very loud.* SMALL JESS, *who is standing on a stool replacing the tins, looks confused.*]

MOTHER: They're fornicating!

[*She rushes to cover up* SMALL JESS's *ears.* SMALL JESS *falls off the stool and the dog starts barking.*]

SMALL JESS: [*Yelling*] Get off!

[*At this moment* ELSIE *comes back in from the toilet and* WILLIAM *appears through the other door wearing his pyjamas.*]

MOTHER: Put some clothes on. Next door are at it again.

[*She's very agitated.*]

MRS GREEN: On a Sunday too!

[*Outside we hear the ice-cream van chime.* MOTHER *lets go of* SMALL JESS *and gets her purse.*]

MOTHER: Go and get five cornets and a wafer for Mrs Green.

[SMALL JESS *takes the money and leaves the room.* MOTHER *wrings her hands.*]

You'd think they could contain themselves on a Sunday.

MAY: Rabbits do as rabbits can.

MRS GREEN: You always said they were like rabbits.

MOTHER: I didn't want Jess to hear this. I don't even let her watch wildlife programmes for fear of what she might see. She doesn't know anything and that's how it should be.

MRS GREEN: The Lord'll stopper up her ears.

ELSIE: She'll have to find out someday.

[*They glare at r ːr: Next door start up again.*]

EXT. STREET. DAY

SMALL JESS *is at the window of the ice-cream van.*

SMALL JESS: They're fornicating next door.

[ICE-CREAM MAN *laughs.*]

What does it mean?

ICE-CREAM MAN: Well, I can't rightly say.

SMALL JESS: Mum says it's a sin but why is it so noisy? Most sins you do quietly so as not to get caught.

[*She takes the ice-cream and trots back into the house, licking as she goes.*]

INT. LIVING ROOM. DAY

MOTHER *is at the piano with* MAY, MRS GREEN *and* ELSIE *gathered round.* SMALL JESS *hands out the ice-cream. She's left with three cornets.*

MOTHER: 'Yield not to Temptation'. Your father's shaving. You can hold mine as well. We're going to sing 'Yield Not To Temptation'. Mrs Green, you be the baritone.

[*They sing the first verse and chorus. At the end of the first verse, the dog is howling and next door are banging on the wall.* MOTHER *pauses.* SMALL JESS *is desperately trying to keep the ice-cream from dripping.*]

MAY: Come on Jess, sing up.

EXT. BACKYARD. DAY

MOTHER *in the backyard, staring over the wall at the just visible head of the eldest boy next door. He's very spotty. We hear her internal prayer.*

MOTHER: The Lord help me to defeat this limb of Satan.

[*He pulls his tongue out at her.*]

[*Yelling*] Hear the Word of the Lord from the Book of Deuteronomy. 'The Lord will smite you with the boils of Egypt and with the ulcers and the scurvy and the itch of which you cannot be cured.'

[*The boy looks very taken aback.*]

INT. LIVING ROOM. DAY

MOTHER *crashes back in through the kitchen and into the living room where* MAY, ELSIE, MRS GREEN *and* DAD *are lined up looking expectant.* SMALL JESS *is bending over her English Gem dictionary.*

MOTHER: Oh, what a triumph! What a day! Jess, aren't you proud of your mother? The Lord gave me the words. I didn't need a dictionary.

[*She goes over and hugs her.*]

SMALL JESS: I was looking up for . . .

[*She is about to say fornication and catches* MAY's *eye and stops.* MOTHER *doesn't seem to have noticed.*]

MRS GREEN: Of course she's proud of you and when she grows up she'll remember this day. The day on which you defeated the Heathen.

MAY: She'll not be like a rabbit.

[MRS GREEN *coughs and looks away but* MOTHER *doesn't appear to have heard.*]

MOTHER: What a triumph! Let me take your photo.

[*They line up while she fiddles with the camera she has got out from the sideboard.*]

SMALL JESS: I don't want to have my photo taken.

MOTHER: When you get older Jess, you'll be glad of photos.

ELSIE: You'll want to look back. Everything changes so fast.

MOTHER: Everything changes but God changes not. Smile!

[*She clicks the camera, the shot freezes into a still.*
The photograph is held in someone's hand. The camera moves up the body to the face and holds there. It is older JESS, *recognisable from the opening fairground scene. The camera spreads and we see* MELANIE *in the shot also looking at the photo.* JESS *smiles at her.*]

JESS: I was seven then . . .

TWO

INT. CHURCH. FANTASY

JESS *and* SMALL JESS *are standing at the back of the church looking towards the front platform where* PASTOR *is standing with his arms upraised and with his back to them. We can only see the backs of the* CONGREGATION. *They are singing 'While I Was Sleeping Somebody Touched Me' in their loud and frenzied way. The usual thumping of tambourines and lots of clapping.*

JESS *and* SMALL JESS *start walking down the aisle towards the platform. They walk slowly as in a dream. From each side of the aisle as they walk, hands stretch out to grab them, though none restrains them. They brush them aside. They reach the platform and stand directly behind* PASTOR. *He swings round suddenly to face them and the music stops. He has the head of a jackal. All the* CONGREGATION *have the heads of animals.* JESS *opens her mouth to scream and as she does so,* SMALL JESS *vanishes and the* CONGREGATION *start to speak in tongues and stamp their feet.*

EXT. MARKET. DAY

JESS *and* ELSIE *giving out tracts and repeating over and over again.*

JESS: Oh, excuse me, can I interest you in the love of Jesus. . . ?

ELSIE: I think you'll find it useful.

JESS: Hope to see you on Sunday. Excuse me can I interest . . . Look, it's Miss Jewsbury.

[MISS JEWSBURY *comes forward smiling.* ELSIE *kisses her.*]

ELSIE: Hello, Jane. I'm worn out with a night of prayer and these two bags of shopping.

MISS JEWSBURY: I've got my car, I'll give you a lift.

ELSIE: Grand. You can come in for a piece of my fruit cake.

[MOTHER *returns.*]

118

MISS JEWSBURY: Been busy with the bargains?

[MOTHER *is very stiff with* MISS JEWSBURY.]

MOTHER: Hello. Hello, Mrs Norris, I see you're helping Jess spread the Word. It's wonderful when the people of the Lord join together.

[*Her body language excludes* MISS JEWSBURY.]

ELSIE: Jane and I will be off now . . .

MISS JEWSBURY: My car's just outside, Elsie, it's not locked. Leave me your bags and I'll be with you in a second. I have to collect something.

ELSIE: Right-o. See you tomorrow, Jess.

[*She nods at* MOTHER *and sets off.*]

JESS: [*To* MISS JEWSBURY] I'll give you a hand if you like.

MOTHER: We're in a hurry, Jess.

[JESS *takes no notice and reaches down to pick up the bags.* MISS JEWSBURY *notices her torn sleeve.*]

MISS JEWSBURY: What happened to your sleeve, Jess?

[*She lifts the dangling sleeve and looks at* MOTHER.]

MOTHER: Oh, she tore it. You know what children are like.

[*She pauses.*]

But I forget, you haven't got any, have you? Not one for family life.

[*As she says this, she's fiddling in her bag for something.* MOTHER *pulls out a roll of Sellotape.*]

MISS JEWSBURY: I can certainly see that Jess is no longer a child. I think she needs a new mac.

MOTHER: We're getting one this afternoon.

[*She starts sellotaping the sleeve on to the body of the mac.*]

JESS: Mum!

MOTHER: Yes, it's hard being a mother.

JESS: Mum!

MOTHER: Don't shout, Jess. Miss Jewsbury's not deaf. She's had her adenoids out.

[*She laughs and looks at* MISS JEWSBURY *who is clearly uncomfortable.*]

MISS JEWSBURY: Well. I'd better be on my way.

MOTHER: We don't see you at church much anymore.

[*She has now sellotaped* JESS *into the mac.*]

MISS JEWSBURY: No. I've found somewhere quieter.

MOTHER: I always thought you were a Methodist.

JESS: Mum!

MOTHER: Will you be quiet? What?

MISS JEWSBURY: I don't think Jess can move her arms.

MOTHER: Oh, have I been over-zealous?

JESS: I'm fed up. I'm going home. I'm going to join the Methodists.

MOTHER: Growing pains, Miss Jewsbury. Goodbye.

> [*To* JESS.]

You're a disgrace. Why did you have to flaunt that mac at her?

JESS: I didn't rip it did I? I'm going home.

> [*She turns to go away.* MOTHER *grabs her and rips off the sleeve entirely.*]

MOTHER: Beezum! To think I brought you all the way from that orphanage for this. They say what's bred in the bone comes out in the marrow.

JESS: Well, I wish you'd left me there.

> [*As she says this* MOTHER *hits her across the face.* JESS *is clearly appalled and recoils.* MOTHER *is flustered.*]

MOTHER: You brought that on yourself. Come on. Let's get you a new mac.

JESS: I want to go home.

MOTHER: Come on.

> [*She pushes her gently. They walk into a stall; cardboard boxes are heaped everywhere, goods spilling out of them. One box has 'surplus' written on the side in huge letters.* MOTHER *starts rummaging in it.*]

MOTHER: I thought that mac'd outlast your father. It would've if it hadn't been for you.

JESS: Those are all too big and I'm not having a pink one. People will laugh at me.

> [MOTHER *pulls out a bright pink mac.*]

MOTHER: Try it on.

> [JESS *puts it on. It's huge.*]

Oh yes. Look, it's even got a hat.

> [*She jams a sou'wester shape on* JESS's *head. It comes low on the crown, almost over her eyes.*]

JESS: It's the wrong way round. It must be. Oh, look, it's too big.

MOTHER: Lovely. You'll grow into it.
JESS: Mum!
MOTHER: We'll take it.

EXT. FISH STALL. DAY

MOTHER *and* JESS *are standing by the fish stall.* JESS *is conspicuous and ridiculous.* FISHMONGER *selling to other customers.*

JESS *lurches around the corner of the fish stall and stares at the bright pink innards of the gutted fish. She looks up and finds herself staring at a very beautiful Pre-Raphaelite looking girl of about seventeen. The girl is in an overall, gutting fish.*]

JESS: I'd like to do that.

[*The girl ignores her.* JESS *coughs and tries again.*]

Everyone looks really miserable don't they? When Keats was miserable he put on a clean shirt . . .

[*The girl looks up with just a flash of interest.*]

But he was a poet . . . Do you work here full time?

MELANIE: Just on Saturdays. I'm doing my A levels. I can't talk to you, they don't like me to have friends at work.

JESS: But I'm not your friend.

MELANIE: I know, but he'll think you are.

JESS: I've got one friend, her name's Elsie, she's 82.

[MELANIE *smiles very faintly and concentrates on her work.*]

I'll come back next week. What's your name?

[*Before* MELANIE *can answer* MOTHER *comes bustling round the fish tank and straightens* JESS's *hat.* JESS *blushes.* MELANIE *drops her head lower.*]

MOTHER: Come on. We're due at Birtwistle's.

JESS: Can I have a fish?

MOTHER: I've got enough to look after what with you and William and that dog.

JESS: Just one.

[MOTHER *ignores her and sets off.* JESS *hovers for a moment and looks at* MELANIE *who says very softly . . .*]

MELANIE: I'm called Melanie.

JESS: I'm Jess.

[*She shoots off to catch up with* MOTHER.]

INT. BIRTWISTLE'S CAFE. DAY

MAY *and* MRS GREEN *are already sitting at the table with mugs in front of them.* MAY *is doing her pools.* MOTHER *is in the process of sitting down as* JESS *rushes in and takes her place at the table.*

MRS GREEN: Oh hello.

MAY: Oh hello.

MRS GREEN: Jess.

[MOTHER *fiddles in her bag and gets out a copy of 'The Band of Hope Review'. She notices* CISSY *in the corner with a mug of tea.*]

MOTHER: Not saved yet, Cissy?

[*She waves 'The Band of Hope Review'.*]

CISSY: Not yet, but still burying them that are.

[*She gets up and collects her things.*]

We've got some old bugger to sink at two o'clock this afternoon. I'd best be off. I could do with a mac like Jess's; nice and voluminous. You'd never credit the mud at a graveside.

MRS GREEN: You can't beat a plastic mac.

MOTHER: I'd be thankful for my graveside. I need something to put an end to my sorrows. Goodbye Cissy.

[*Exit* CISSY.]

MAY: Have a Horlicks. Nettie! Nettie!

[NETTIE, *the waitress, comes over. It turns out to be* MRS ARKWRIGHT. *She's smoking a cigarette and her glasses are askew, at an angle, and stuck together with band aid.*]

MOTHER: Mrs Arkwright. What are you doing here?

MRS ARKWRIGHT: No business, that's what. I can't keep a proper home going on vermin alone. I've had to come waitressing. What can I get for you?

MOTHER: Horlicks for me and a milk shake for Jess.

JESS: Banana, please.

MAY: Hey, what's happened to yer specs? They weren't like that just now?

MRS ARKWRIGHT: Oooh, that Irene dropped her delivery o' beef burgers on 'em. I'd just taken 'em off to wipe me eyes . . .

[MRS ARKWRIGHT *starts flicking her cloth over the table while* MOTHER *recoils.*]

MRS ARKWRIGHT: And she slammed them things down and now look. As if I haven't enough expense.

[*She takes them off and stares at them ruefully.*]

MAY: What do you reckon to Liverpool versus Rovers?

MRS ARKWRIGHT: Nowt. They freeze them things just like bricks nowadays. I like a fridge but you can go too far with progress. It's progress what's ruining my business. You can't keep bugs down forever.

MOTHER: Can I have my Horlicks?

MRS ARKWRIGHT: People think they've got rid of them, but they mutate.

[*To* JESS.]

Do you want a Saturday job?

JESS: What doing?

MRS ARKWRIGHT: Washing glasses.

MOTHER: Yes, she does.

[JESS *smiles.*]

EXT. FISH STALL. DAY

JESS *is hovering by the fish stall. She's not in her mac. It's another time.* MELANIE *is nowhere in sight.* JESS *is clearly put out. She walks over to the* FISHMONGER *and asks with some hesitancy:*

JESS: Is Melanie ill?

FISHMONGER: Oh, it's you again. No, last week was her finish. You can start here if you fancy. You've been hanging around long enough to know what to do. I'll give you three pounds for the day and a kipper to take home.

[*He holds up a dripping trout.* JESS *shakes her head and turns away. She turns straight into* MELANIE.]

JESS: You've left!

MELANIE: I've got a job at the library. The money's better. Mum and me need it.

JESS: I've been here every week . . .

MELANIE: I know.

JESS: But it's always too busy to talk.

MELANIE: I know.

[*She smiles uncertainly. There is an awkward pause.*]

JESS: Have you got time for a baked potato?

[MELANIE *nods*.]

EXT. MARKET. DAY

JESS *and* MELANIE *are walking through market. They find a bench and sit down.*

JESS: I work at Birtwistle's Caff; you could come and get a milk shake when you finish.

MELANIE: I haven't enough money.

JESS: *No*, it's free. I'll say you're my friend.

MELANIE: I don't know many people round here. We used to live in Halifax. We live in a council house up by the cemetery now, but at least we've got our own bathroom. We didn't have before.

JESS: We've got one too now. My Mum built it.

MELANIE: I didn't know there were women plumbers.

JESS: She's not a plumber. No, she found this toilet in our back alley and just as she was planting out her geraniums in it, the Lord told her she had Do-It-Yourself skills and that she should build us a bathroom.

MELANIE: Are you religious?

JESS: Yes, but we're not boring. You see Jesus does things for us. It's just like having a friend who always wants to see you.

MELANIE: I'd like that.

[*There is a short pause.* JESS *gathers herself.*]

JESS: Well, why don't you come to our church then? You can have your own tambourine.

MELANIE: Oh, I'm Catholic.

JESS: Oh well, God doesn't mind. Come tomorrow.

MELANIE: I'll have to ask my mum.

JESS: Oh, you can bring her. And your Dad.

MELANIE: I haven't got a Dad. That's why I have to save all my money if I want to go to college. Mum's money is all for the housekeeping.

JESS: Oh, well, I haven't got one either. [*She pauses*] Well, not much . . .

[MELANIE *looks at her in confusion.*]

He's quiet, but he's deep. The Lord speaks to him silently. My mum though, she's different. Oh, well, you'll see.

EXT. CHURCH. DAY

The faithful are gathered on the pavement outside the church. There is a general sense of excitement and milling around. WILLIAM *is standing in the doorway holding a great pile of hymn books which he gives out as people go past.*

MOTHER, MAY, MRS GREEN, ELSIE, JESS *and* MELANIE *are grouped together. Suddenly a car drives by. The windows are open. One man sticks his head out and shouts:* 'Holy Joes – use your Bibles to wipe your bums. Hey, have you got any Brides of Christ who fancy a bit? Holy Joes!'

MRS GREEN: On a Sunday too.

MOTHER: Sent by the Devil, they were. They used to live by the Glue Works on the Factory Bottoms. You know, near that Arkwright woman and just opposite the pea cannery. Then their cousin died and left them a house next to us. Yes, my next door neighbours, Mrs Green. Limbs of Satan all.

[*While* MOTHER *makes this speech,* MAY *is behind her mouthing it over her shoulder.* MRS GREEN *is nodding and trying not to smile. Suddenly as she finishes,* MOTHER *wheels round.*]

MAY: Well, we have heard it before.

MOTHER: Don't mock, May. I've had it hard. The Lord knows how hard.

MRS GREEN: He does, he does. I see Jess has brought a friend. That's nice.

MOTHER: She's not saved yet. I won't let Jess have friends who aren't saved. She's getting rebellious.

MAY: Think of your reward in heaven.

MOTHER: I'll have a mansion.

MAY: You will and none of your clothes will be second-hand.

[MOTHER *turns to protest but at that moment an old Bedford van draws up in front of them. The* PASTOR *leaps out looking manic.*]

PASTOR: Here it is! Bought with the money you all gave. Here it is. The Glory Bus.

[*As the faithful walk around it, we see that on one side is a picture of the Terrified Damned and on the other, the Heavenly Host.*

CONGREGATION *all ad lib.*

ELSIE *and* OTHERS *are standing at the back of the bus where, in green lettering, is inscribed: 'Heaven or Hell'.*

The PASTOR *comes hurrying round and flings open the back doors.* MAY, MRS GREEN *and* MOTHER *crowd behind.*]

PASTOR: You see? I have a collapsible cross and a first-aid kit in case I'm casting out demons and we have an accident. I've seen people combust.

ELSIE: What do you do about the flames?

PASTOR: I use an extinguisher.

[*He waves a small portable extinguisher while the crowd makes admiring noises.*]

Yes, and I have a small sink with running water. Just as Jesus bade the possessed swine leap into the Gadarene Sea, so I rinse the demon with this tap.

[*He steps out and closes the doors.*]

And the last of the signs and wonders is my salvation flag which can hoist from the cockpit whenever I want to raise a salute to Jesus.

[*He leans in the driver's seat, fiddles about and a flag pops up on the top of the van.*]

JESS: Amazing.

PASTOR: Jess, I'm glad you're here. I want you to look after Graham. This is Graham.

[GRAHAM *appears round the van. He's good-looking and rather shy.*]

PASTOR: He's only just accepted Christ as his Saviour. He'll be coming to our church from now on and I want you to steer him in the way.

[MAY *comes butting in briefly.*]

MAY: Just right, eh Jess?

[*She vanishes again.* JESS *takes no notice. The* PASTOR *puts one arm on* GRAHAM'S *shoulder and the other on* JESS'S.]

JESS: Hello Graham. I'm Jess. I take the Bible Study class on Mondays. You should come to that.

[GRAHAM *nods and says nothing. He looks at* PASTOR.]

GRAHAM: Shall I bring in my guitar?

PASTOR: Yes, yes, the Psalmist said, 'Make a joyful noise unto the Lord.'

[*As* GRAHAM *turns away to go into the van,* PASTOR *draws* JESS *aside a little and lowers his voice.*]

Remember your body is a temple, Jess. Don't give in to temptation. He's a good-looking boy isn't he?

[JESS *stares at the floor. The* PASTOR *laughs.*]

JESS: We'll be like Jane Eyre and St John Rivers. That's Mum's favourite book.

PASTOR: And the Bible, eh Jess?

[MOTHER *comes and joins them and looks at* JESS *closely and at the back view of* GRAHAM *getting his stuff out of the van.*]

MOTHER: Never mind the flesh Jess, think of the spirit . . .

[*She crosses over to* GRAHAM *and helps him with his things.* PASTOR *ushers everyone into the church.*

JESS *goes over to* MELANIE *who's standing out of it all and looking worried.*]

JESS: Trust me.

[MELANIE *nods and looks closely at* JESS. *She is trusting her.*]

INT. CHURCH: DAY

MELANIE *and* JESS *are sitting beside* ELSIE *and* MAY. MOTHER *is at the piano.* PASTOR *is on the platform, a pair of bongos beside him.* GRAHAM *is there, too, with his guitar.*

PASTOR: Before we sing our last hymn I'd like to share with you a little of what Jesus has been doing through me this week. You know it's my special ministry to recognise the demon and to cast out that fiend.

[*As he says this he smashes his fist into his palm. There are appreciative murmurs and Amens from the* CONGREGATION.]

Even now, as we sit here today drinking in the Word of the Lord, there is an epidemic of demons, spreading through the North West. Lancashire and Cheshire are the worst. Only yesterday I cleansed a whole family in Cheadle Hume. Ridden they were. Yes, ridden. And do you know why?

127

[*The whole* CONGREGATION *has fallen silent.* PASTOR's *eyes roam the chairs.* MELANIE *looks like she's going to be sick.*]

PASTOR: *Unnatural Passions!*

[MOTHER *bangs a chromatic chord on the piano and shouts out* 'Lord forgive them!']

And now I'd like to ask Jess to come and lead us in a chorus and a word of prayer while I walk amongst you laying hands on any who need the touch of the Lord. For some are sick and some are sad and some have lost the joy they had . . .

[*He gets down from the platform and goes walkabout.*

JESS *takes his place and lifts up her hands. She's radiant.*]

JESS: Let us sing to the Lord. Let us give our thanks to Jesus who died for us and has risen again and is with us still. Let's sing 'Somebody Touched Me' and do our best for Jesus as he has done his best for us.

[MOTHER *starts playing the piano. The boys join in.* JESS *picks up the bongos and sings loudly. Soon the singing and jumping about becomes as frenzied as in Jess's dream.* MAY *passes* MELANIE *a tambourine.* MELANIE *looks appalled.*]

MAY: Let the spirit in, Melanie.

MELANIE: Let it in where?

[*As the chorus comes to an end* JESS *holds up her hands again.* MOTHER *twists around and realises that she isn't going to do another round and, instead, starts playing a much quieter chorus: 'He Touched Me'.*]

JESS: In a moment we'll have a word of prayer. And if there's any among us who hasn't yet given their life to Jesus, put aside doubt and fear and the things of the past and use tonight to start your future. Your future as a child of God with a mansion in the sky.

MAY: Amen, amen.

[*She beams at* MELANIE.]

JESS: Let's sing, 'He Touched Me'. And if you don't know the words, sing along as best you can.

[EVERYONE *starts singing.*]

'He touched me, He touched me,

And oh the joy that filled my soul.

Something happened, and now I know,

He touched me and made me whole.'
[PASTOR *comes back on to the platform while this is going on and whispers to* JESS *who goes back to her seat.*]

PASTOR: I know there's someone out there waiting to give their life to Jesus. Put your hand in the air and let me know so that I can pray for you.

[JESS *smiles at* MELANIE; PASTOR *looks straight in her direction. Tentatively* MELANIE *puts her hand in the air.*]

PASTOR: I see your hand!

MAY: Hallelujah.

ELSIE: Amen Jesus.

MRS GREEN: Another sheep in the fold.

MOTHER: What a little lamb!

[MOTHER *and* MRS GREEN *shake hands as if making a deal.*]

INT. KITCHEN. DAY

MOTHER *and* JESS *are in the kitchen. The kettle is steaming.*
MOTHER *is cutting something out of* The Plain Truth. JESS *is rolling pastry.*

MOTHER: Get that pastry properly flat.

JESS: I hate cooking.

MOTHER: So do I. If it wasn't for you and your Dad, I'd be a missionary. It's too hot to cook, out there. They just eat pineapples all the time. Hurry up, I want to talk to you about something.

JESS: What? I wouldn't mind a pineapple. I've been eating oranges for sixteen years. It's unnatural.

MOTHER: I want to talk to you about boys.

[*She finishes cutting out and gives it to* JESS.]

MOTHER: You can give this cutting to Melanie. It's from *The Plain Truth* and it's all about being a new Christian.

JESS: What about boys?

MOTHER: I saw the way you were looking at Graham when he came to our church. It's only natural, a nice boy like that, but . . .

JESS: I wasn't looking at him. I was saying hello to him. I was looking after Melanie.

MOTHER: That's different. I've prayed about this and the Lord told me to tell you the story of Pierre and how I nearly came to a bad end.

JESS: Pierre!

INT. PARLOUR. DAY

MOTHER *and* JESS *huddle close with their cups of tea and a packet of biscuits. Very soft concertina music in the background.*

MOTHER: When I was young I was headstrong and I got a job teaching in Paris. I lived off the Boulevard St Germain, ate croissants and lived a clean life. I wasn't with the Lord then but I had high standards. Then, one sunny day, when I wasn't expecting it, I met Pierre. Or should I say Pierre met me. He jumped off his bicycle, offering me his onions and said I was the most beautiful woman he had ever seen.

[MOTHER *pats* JESS's *hair.*]

JESS: Gosh!

MOTHER: Naturally I was flattered.

JESS: Then what?

MOTHER: I'm telling you . . . Well, we exchanged addresses and he started taking me out to restaurants and night clubs so that we could dance till the small hours while the waiters were folding up the checked table-cloths and saying 'Alors' to each other. On those nights I started to feel a sort of giddiness and a fizzing and a buzzing in my stomach – in the pit of my stomach. [*She pauses*] The very pit. I thought it must be love, but there was no reason to be in love. I mean, Pierre wasn't handsome like the men in the magazines or like Pastor Spratt. But the feeling wouldn't go away. Then, one night, after a quiet supper and a romantic walk along the banks of the moonlit Seine, Pierre clasped me to him and begged me. His very words were 'Voulez-vous couchez avec moi, ce soir?'

JESS: What does that mean?

MOTHER: [*All coy*] Well, roughly speaking it means: Don't go home without me.

JESS: Oh.

MOTHER: [*Suddenly overcome*] Lord forgive me, but I did it.

[MOTHER *stops, overcome with emotion.* JESS *encourages her to continue with the offer of a biscuit.*]

MOTHER: The worst is still to come.

[*Leaving a pregnant pause as she chews on her biscuit.*]

A few days later I went to the Doctor for a check-up. I told him about the fizzing and buzzing and explained to him that I was in love and so I needed a bit of help. You know, medical help. [*She adds heavy emphasis to the words.*]

He started frowning and humming and after he'd examined me and washed his hands he said: [*She mimics a French accent*] 'You may be, love, but you also have ze stomach ulcer!'

[*She pauses, overcome with feeling.* JESS *pats her hand.*]

Imagine Jess, I had given away my all for an ailment.

JESS: Then am I. . . ?

MOTHER: There was no issue.

[JESS *stands up slowly and picks up Mother's cutting. She kisses her* MOTHER.]

MOTHER: So just you take care. What you think is the heart might well be another organ.

JESS: Thank you. I'd better get over to Elsie's. Melanie will be waiting for me.

[*She's fantastically embarrassed. As* JESS *is going out the back door* MOTHER *calls.* JESS *turns.*]

MOTHER: Don't let any boy touch you 'Down There'.

[*She points to the level of her apron pocket.* JESS *stares at the warning hand.*]

INT. PARLOUR. ELSIE'S HOUSE. NIGHT

ELSIE *comes in with two filled hot water bottles.* JESS *and* MELANIE *are making up a bed on the sofa and a bed on the floor. We see the fireplace and Jess's sampler, 'The summer is ended and we are not yet saved', framed over it. Everything is warm and friendly.*

ELSIE: It is nice having you two stay the night. I feel safe. The world's full of robbers.

JESS: Jesus will protect you, Elsie.

ELSIE: He will when my mind's on him but we're having a rest

131

from each other just now. He goes his way and I go mine. If not,
I'll never get those skirting boards painted.

MELANIE: Is that scriptural?

[JESS *shakes her head.*]

ELSIE: The Lord has his ways and I have mine.

[*She chuckles and holds up the hot water bottles.*]

Well now, come on you two. I can't stay up for ever.

JESS: Melanie wants to be a missionary. I wish I did.

ELSIE: Why don't you?

JESS: Because I don't like hot places. I got sunstroke in
Morecambe last year.

ELSIE: You don't have to do everything your mother tells you.
Now, bed.

INT. LIVING ROOM. ELSIE'S HOUSE. NIGHT

MELANIE *and* JESS *lying together on the floor in front of the fire.
The sofa hasn't been used. There's a large Bible close to them. The
only light is from the fire.*

JESS *is lying flat on her back, covers pulled up.* MELANIE *is
leaning over her slightly, propping her head on her hand. Her
mane of hair glitters in the candlelight.*]

MELANIE: I was lonely before I met you.

JESS: I was lonely too. Mum don't let me have friends unless
they're saved. I haven't got any friends at school. Not real ones.

MELANIE: We're like David and Jonathan in the Bible. They were
married but they loved each other best. It says so.

JESS: And when we're married we'll still love each other best.

MELANIE: I don't want to get married.

[MELANIE *rolls over and lies on her back staring at the ceiling.*]

JESS: Why not?

MELANIE: You have to cook and clean all the time.

JESS: When I was little the first fairy story that I ever read was
Beauty and the Beast. Do you remember it?

MELANIE: Yeah.

JESS: And then May told me that she had married a pig and
because he looked just like one, all squinty eyed and red-
skinned, I thought that she meant it.

MELANIE: What, really?

JESS: Yes, really. And then I kept looking at all the men like this horrible man in the butcher's and wondering if they were beasts. And I thought that most of the women in our street had done pretty badly.

[MELANIE *starts laughing.*]

And I thought how disappointed they must be if they'd married their beast and they'd started kissing them and nothing happened.

[MELANIE *is now rolling around with laughter.* JESS *is laughing too, but controlling herself.*]

JESS: I thought that all over the world in all innocence, women were marrying beasts.

[JESS *starts tickling* MELANIE, *who laughs even more. They're rolling around, the covers thrown back. Both are naked.* MELANIE *is half-lying on top of* JESS. *Suddenly she kisses her, fierce and short. They look at each other.* MELANIE *bends and kisses* JESS *again, for a long time.* JESS's *hand strokes the length of her back.*]

INT. ELSIE'S BEDROOM. ELSIE'S HOUSE. NIGHT

A shot of ELSIE *lying in bed, her false teeth beside her on the table.*

INT. MOTHER'S BEDROOM. NIGHT

A shot of MOTHER *lying awake reading the Bible.*

INT. PARLOUR. ELSIE'S HOUSE. NIGHT

A shot of the fire, now burnt low. JESS *and* MELANIE *are lying sideways on, looking at each other.*

MELANIE: I went out with a boy once. All he did was push me against the back fence and wriggle a lot. That was horrible.

JESS: I've never had a boyfriend. The beasts put me off. Graham's not a beast but he's boring.

MELANIE: Don't tell me about the beasts again. You make me laugh.

[JESS *rolls* MELANIE *on to her stomach and sits astride her back.*]

JESS: Look! Over there!

[*Camera on the wall where* JESS *makes the following shadows.*]

JESS: There are men in the world. Then there are the women in the world and then there are the beasts.

[*She makes a roaring noise and has her shadowy beast rage over the wall.* MELANIE *laughs, wriggles over and gets out of bed. She goes and stands by the window. The curtains are open, it's coming light.*]

MELANIE: Come and see.

[JESS *walks over and joins her. They stand at the window, their backs towards the camera, their arms round each other, looking out over the street.*]

JESS: This can't be unnatural passion, can it?

INT. BIRTWISTLE'S CAFE. DAY

MELANIE *and* JESS *in the cafe.* MRS ARKWRIGHT *floating about.* JESS *is clearing tables.* MELANIE *is having a milk shake. Sonny and Cher in the background singing 'I Got You Babe'.*

JESS: Have you just finished?

MELANIE: Yes, it was early closing at the library today. They're stock-taking. Shall we go to Elsie's tonight? My mum's on nights.

JESS: I can't. Mum wants me to stay in.

MELANIE: Why?

JESS: I don't know, she don't normally mind me seeing you. But this morning she asked me to come home straight after work.

MELANIE: Is it something to do with me? I thought she liked me?

JESS: She does, I know she does.

[MRS ARKWRIGHT *comes by and plonks another milk shake down.*]

MRS ARKWRIGHT: Here, nipper, sit down for five minutes. Stop pretending to work.

[*She goes off without waiting for a response.*]

JESS: She'll be all right soon, she's just moody. She didn't talk to my Dad for nearly a year once, and then he stopped talking to her. [*She pauses.*] Or anybody else.

MELANIE: Will you walk home with me then? I'll wait for you?

JESS: Better not.

> [MELANIE *nods. She's unhappy.*]

She'll be all right soon. You're just not used to her.

INT. KITCHEN/LIVING ROOM, EARLY EVENING

A few weeks later. JESS *and* MOTHER *in the living room standing by a huge collection of paint tins and paint paraphernalia.* JESS *is in a pair of overalls. She's putting old paint tins into bin bags.* MOTHER *is tying up clean brushes with string. Glimpse of* DAD *watching television with the sound turned down.*

JESS: I haven't been out for three weeks, except to go to church and school. We can't do any more painting. There's nothing left to paint. We've done the skirting boards twice and I've whitewashed the coal-house every night this week because you said it was streaky. Now it looks like a Greek Temple.

MOTHER: Don't start heathen talk with me.

JESS: I'm not. But you said you wanted me to help and now we've finished. So I'm going round to Elsie's.

MOTHER: What for?

JESS: Because I like her. Because I always go on Saturdays.

MOTHER: And Melanie goes too.

> [MOTHER *gets up and goes into the kitchen.* JESS *follows her.* MOTHER *starts putting dirty brushes into glass jars to soak.*]

MOTHER: You used to like staying in with your Dad and me.

JESS: I do like staying in with you. [*She tries to hug* MOTHER *and gets shrugged off.*] I'll see you at church in the morning.

> [MOTHER *drops the jam jars.* JESS *bends down to help her pick them up. They're broken.*]

MOTHER: Just leave it. Go if you're going.

JESS: I'm not in a hurry. [*She continues to clear up.*]

MOTHER: I said leave it.

JESS: What's the matter? You don't usually drop things.

MOTHER: I'm bad with my nerves.

JESS: You haven't got any nerves.

> [*Again she reaches out to* MOTHER *affectionately.* MOTHER *is rougher this time.*]

135

JESS: Now what have I said? [*She pauses.*] Is there anything you want me to take to Elsie?

MOTHER: [*Bitterly*] I'm sure you and Melanie have thought of everything.

[*She passes back through the living room where* DAD *is still sitting. As she passes she kisses him on the top of his head.*]

EXT. GRAVEYARD. NIGHT

JESS *in the graveyard gathering flowers. A few from each grave. It's getting dark. Suddenly* CISSY *appears beside her, a pair of shears in her hand.*

CISSY: What's this then? I should report you.

JESS: Flowers from the dead to the living.

CISSY: Come over 'ere, there's some lovely roses.

[*They walk to a grave near by.* CISSY *stoops to get* JESS *some flowers.*]

I've gone in with Joe now, that undertaker who used to work for Gloomy Alf. We've got our own parlour now, just by the cemetery. We're doing well. You should come and see us.

JESS: I will.

[*She takes the flowers as* CISSY *hands them to her.*]

CISSY: How's your mother?

JESS: She doesn't like me anymore.

CISSY: Don't be silly. It's always the way with families. She loves you.

JESS: I told her I didn't want to be a missionary.

[CISSY *stands up and rearranges* JESS*'s bundle.*]

CISSY: Why should you be? Daft job anyway. Are these for her?

JESS: No. They're for my friend, Melanie. She likes flowers but she can't afford them.

CISSY: Well you'd best be quick if you're walking through the graveyard. Joe'll be locking the gates at the other end.

JESS: I'll climb over.

CISSY: No respect.

[*She cuffs* JESS *jokingly and walks with her along the path.*]
Come soon. I never did show you how to make a wreath.

[CISSY *stands still, shears in hand as* JESS *continues on her way,*

her arms full of flowers. JESS *half turns back and calls.*]
JESS: Thanks for the flowers.
  [*She starts to run down the path.* CISSY *watches and sighs. It's almost dark.*]

EXT. ELSIE'S FRONT DOOR. NIGHT

JESS *knocks on* ELSIE's *door.* MELANIE *answers it.* JESS *goes inside and gives her the flowers.*

INT. JESS'S BEDROOM. NIGHT

MOTHER *is going through* JESS's *books and drawers. She picks up a musical box and finds more letters. All the letters and suspect books get thrown on to the bed.* WILLIAM *is standing by the door looking unhappy.*
MOTHER: If you're not going to help me, William, go downstairs. There's the kitchen cupboard to mend. I'm protecting her, William. It's Jess I'm protecting.
  [WILLIAM *nods and goes.* MOTHER *picks the letters and books off the bed.*]

INT. CHURCH. DAY

The CONGREGATION *are assembled, singing a hymn.* JESS, MELANIE *and* ELSIE *roll in late and slither into their seats.* MOTHER *glances at them and looks away. The hymn finishes and everyone sits down.*
PASTOR: There is a prayer we say, you all know it. 'Some are sick and some are sad and some have lost the joy they had.' This morning we are praying for two of our number like that. This morning I have a hard task ahead.
  [MOTHER *walks out to the front looking awful.*]
There are two of our number have committed a great sin. A terrible sin. The sin that dare not speak its name.
  [*He pauses and looks around.*]
Jess, Melanie. Come to the front please.
  [MISS JEWSBURY *who is sitting behind leans forward and hisses.*]

MISS JEWSBURY: Keep calm, keep calm.

[JESS *and* MELANIE *get up and walk slowly to the front. They are holding hands. Both are ashen.* PASTOR *stands behind them on the platform and places a hand on each of their necks.*]

PASTOR: These children of God have fallen foul of their lusts. Their bodies have proved stronger than their spirits, their hearts are fixed on carnal things.

[MOTHER *starts to weep.* MRS GREEN *goes up and comforts her.*] These children are full of demons.

[*A ripple of horror runs through the* CONGREGATION.]

JESS: [*Loudly*] I'm not and neither is she.

PASTOR: [*Shouting*] Be quiet!

JESS: I said it's not true.

[PASTOR *hits her about the head and tightens his grip.*]

PASTOR: Now we hear the voice of the demon arguing with the voice of the Lord. Now we hear Satan's voice. Do you deny that you love this young woman with a love reserved for husband and wife?

JESS: Yes – no, it's not like that.

PASTOR: St Paul says in Romans, Chapter One, 'Claiming to be wise they became fools. Therefore God gave them up to the lusts of their hearts. To the dishonouring of their bodies among themselves. Their women exchanged natural relations for unnatural, receiving in the end the due penalty for error.'

[MELANIE *starts crying and falls to her knees, the* PASTOR *goes down after her.* JESS *stands free.*]

JESS: St Paul says in Romans, Chapter Fourteen, 'I know and am persuaded in the Lord that nothing is unnatural in itself; it is made unnatural by those who think it is unnatural.'

[PASTOR *ignores her and pays attention to* MELANIE *who is hysterical with fear.*]

PASTOR: Do you truly repent of your sin and put it behind you forever?

MELANIE: [*Through her sobs*] Yes. Yes.

MOTHER/MRS GREEN: Praise the Lord.

PASTOR: Praise the Lord. Go to the vestry with Mrs Green and Jess's mother. It's not too late for those who truly repent.

[*As* MELANIE *staggers to her feet aided by* MRS GREEN *and*

MOTHER, JESS *takes her face in both hands.*]

JESS: I love you.

[MELANIE *says nothing, but howls afresh and is led away.* JESS *turns to* PASTOR.]

I love her.

PASTOR: Then you do not love the Lord.

[*Suddenly* ELSIE *stands up from the* CONGREGATION.]

ELSIE: Are you trying to help this child or hurt her?

PASTOR: Don't interrupt me, Elsie.

ELSIE: I said are you trying to help this child or hurt her?

[*She starts coughing and falls on to the chair in front.* WILLIAM *rushes to help her. There is a general worry and fuss.* PASTOR *goes down to see her. Suddenly* JESS *sees* MISS JEWSBURY *beckoning. She leaves the church at her sign. No-one notices.*]

INT. PARLOUR. ELSIE'S HOUSE. DAY

JESS *on the sofa.* MISS JEWSBURY *comes to sit beside her.*

MISS JEWSBURY: Why weren't you careful, Jess?

JESS: Careful about what?

MISS JEWSBURY: How you were together? Anybody could see what you were about. It was all over your faces.

JESS: Love's like that. You can't hide love.

MISS JEWSBURY: You'll have to learn.

JESS: I'll never learn to hide what's good. What have they done to her?

MISS JEWSBURY: She'll be all right. She won't argue.

JESS: She loves me.

MISS JEWSBURY: I think you'd better stay here tonight. You're not ready for them.

JESS: Mum will worry.

MISS JEWSBURY: She'll guess where you are. She knows you've got a key. Elsie's been trying to protect you. When she started to get ill she asked me to take over. That's why I'm here. Come on now, you must rest.

[JESS *and* MISS JEWSBURY *stand up.* MISS JEWSBURY *goes to a cupboard and gets out a brandy bottle and glass.*]

JESS: I don't understand.

MISS JEWSBURY: It's my problem too.

JESS: What?

MISS JEWSBURY: Loving the wrong people.

INT. HALL/PARLOUR. DAY

Morning. JESS *trying to sneak down the hall past the parlour. As she gets to the parlour door it flies open. The* PASTOR *is standing there.*

PASTOR: Jess. We've been waiting for you. Jesus has been waiting for you.

JESS: I've got to go to school.

[*She sees* MAY, MRS GREEN *and* MOTHER. *A pot of tea and a few cups are spread out.* MOTHER *pours* JESS *a cup and passes it to her.*]

MOTHER: Where did you spend the night?

JESS: How's Elsie?

PASTOR: She's in hospital.

MOTHER: At Miss Jewsbury's I'll bet.

MRS GREEN: She's not holy.

[*She sips her tea.*]

JESS: Where's Melanie?

PASTOR: She's resting after her ordeal.

JESS: What ordeal?

PASTOR: You.

MAY: Oh, she's safe, don't fret. She's come back to Jesus now.

[JESS *sits down, holding her tea.* MOTHER *butters a piece of toast and gives it to her.*]

JESS: [*Grinning suddenly*] There'll be no breakfasts in hell.

PASTOR: We're doing this for your own good.

MAY: It's because we want to help you.

PASTOR: We've never talked much have we?

MRS GREEN: It's your attitude.

PASTOR: Sit up straight please.

JESS: Can I go now?

MAY: We're here to help you.

PASTOR: We've watched and prayed all night long. And now

we're going to pray over you. We're going to get the demons out of you, Jess.

JESS: I haven't got a demon.

PASTOR: Have you got the cords of love?

[*He stands up and goes over to* MOTHER *who takes soft red ropes out of her bag.*]

JESS: What are they for? Are you going to hurt me?

[*She stands up and makes for the door, but* MRS GREEN *is already standing by it.*]

PASTOR: No one's going to hurt you, Jess. It's the demon we want to hurt.

MRS GREEN: Amen. Amen Jesus.

JESS: No, no.

PASTOR: Lie down, Jess.

[*He uncoils the ropes and shows them to her.*]

PASTOR: These are the cords of love.

JESS: No! No!

[*As she shouts the three women grab her and push her to the floor.* MAY *sits on her legs while* MOTHER *and* MRS GREEN *hold her shoulders down. All the time* JESS *is shouting and struggling.*]

MAY: Be quiet, Jess. I don't want to be hurting you. She's strong.

MRS GREEN: Strong as the devil inside her.

[PASTOR *bends down and ties her feet together.*]

PASTOR: You can't run away, Jess. Remember what the Psalmist said, 'Whither shall I flee from thy spirit?' This room is full of angels in invisible dress. A room full of angels, one devil. You'll soon be free. Jess.

JESS: Get off me. Mum, get him off me. Mum!

MOTHER: Hush. It's the Lord's work.

PASTOR: I've tied them tight Jess, but not for long. Turn her over please ladies.

[*They roll* JESS *over and* PASTOR *ties her hands together behind her back.*]

PASTOR: My National Service training still comes in useful. Now Jess, I want you to think about Jesus.

MAY: Think about his goodness and his loving kindness.

JESS: There's no kindness here. I hate you all.

[*She twists over and looks at* MOTHER.]

JESS: And I hate you most of all.

MRS GREEN: Filth. Devil's filth from her mouth. It's what comes of raising an orphan. Well, a bastard really.

JESS: I'm not the bastard.

PASTOR: I think we'd better use the gag. I don't want to hear this. It will get much worse as the demon struggles for supremacy.

MOTHER: Don't.

[PASTOR *kneels over* JESS's *body, one leg either side, and gazes on her. He fiddles in his pockets and comes out with a clean, folded handkerchief which he shakes out carefully while* JESS *watches.* MOTHER *is kneeling behind* JESS's *head.* MAY *and* MRS GREEN *are standing on either side.*]

PASTOR: She's so pretty. Sometimes the devil scars you as he comes free. You might be scarred, Jess. You might not be pretty anymore.

[*He reaches down to stroke her face. She bites him very hard. He yelps.* MOTHER *hits* JESS *across the face. Immediately,* PASTOR *gags her. She is trussed up and helpless. She looks at him.*]

PASTOR: Let me tell you what's going to happen, Jess.

[*He continues to straddle her, nursing his wounded finger as he talks.*]

PASTOR: We're going to pray over you for seven hours. Not May and Mrs Green and your mother all the time. I've arranged for a team to work shifts. It's exhausting you know, our struggle against the demon, but you see how much we love you. For three days and three nights you must live in this room and think about Jesus. Not soft bodies and easy pleasure, but the virtues of your Saviour. This may sound harsh Jess, but it's softer than hell. I've never known the demon last against us for more than three days.

MOTHER: We're doing this for you, Jess.

[*She tries to stroke* JESS's *head.* JESS *grunts and twists away as best she can but* MOTHER *continues.*]

PASTOR: Let's start our intercession. Now, Jess, I want you to think about the crucified Christ and his sacrifice for you. If you think of Jesus's suffering, how can you consider your own?

MAY: Amen. Amen. Oh, Lord, come down among us. End this girl's suffering.
[*They all start to pray. Their voices carry over into the beginning of the next scene.*]

EXT. HILL TOP. DAY

JESS *tightly wrapped up on the hill with the dog.* MISS JEWSBURY *is with her.*

JESS: Stand behind the trees. Mum can see up here with her binoculars.

MISS JEWSBURY: Are you all right, Jess?

JESS: No. I want you to find Melanie and give her this letter.
[*She fumbles in her coat pocket and brings out a letter.*]

JESS: I've got to see her.

MISS JEWSBURY: I don't know about that, Jess.

JESS: You know, while they had me locked up, towards the end, I thought I saw a demon. An orange one.

MISS JEWSBURY: You don't mean that. You were ill.

JESS: I do mean that. It wasn't bad, it wasn't a demon the way Pastor talks about them. This one looked like me but it glowed all fiery with orange hair and it told me that I had to make a choice.

MISS JEWSBURY: You do, Jess. You have to follow the Lord.

JESS: You hate it here. They hate you here. Why don't you go away?

MISS JEWSBURY: Where to? It's the same wherever you go.

JESS: It's not! It can't be! You've got to fight.

MISS JEWSBURY: Go home now, Jess. They'll be wondering.

JESS: Promise about the letter?

MISS JEWSBURY: Promise.
[JESS *kisses her lightly and sets off down the hill.* MISS JEWSBURY *watches. Suddenly* JESS *turns round.*]

JESS: You've got to fight.
[*She shouts this through cupped hands and runs off. Camera on* MISS JEWSBURY *for a second. Her eyes are full of tears.*]

EXT. DOOR OUTSIDE MELANIE'S HOUSE. NIGHT

JESS *at the front door.* MELANIE *appears, sees who it is and starts to shut the door.*

JESS: Listen, girl, don't do that! Say goodbye to me very loudly, let me sneak upstairs, you come up as soon as you can. Miss Jewsbury's outside, she'll wait for me till morning.

[MELANIE *hesitates.* JESS *grabs her hand.*]

Do it! This is me you're turning away.

INT. BEDROOM, MELANIE'S HOUSE. NIGHT

JESS *is curled up with* MELANIE. *A candle burns by the bed. As they talk,* MELANIE *strokes* JESS'S *hair.*

MELANIE: Did they hurt you?

JESS: Yes. Did they hurt you?

MELANIE: No, I didn't fight.

JESS: You know some of the things we talked about, like about the future, what we might do. They're things I won't forget, things I'll do. Go to university, go away maybe. I never even thought about leaving home before I met you.

MELANIE: I've made it a mess for you.

JESS: No, you haven't. No. You've made it different, better. You don't wish it hadn't happened. Do you?

MELANIE: No.

JESS: Make love to me.

MELANIE: I can't, I can't.

JESS: Well, then I'll make love to you. Let the sin be mine.

[*They start to make love.*]

PASTOR: [*Voice over*] A soul redeemed for Jesus.

INT. PARLOUR. DAY

PASTOR, JESS, MOTHER, MAY, MRS GREEN. WILLIAM *is handing around cups of tea.*

PASTOR: Don't you feel better Jess?

MOTHER: She does, you can tell.

MAY: She looks like her old self again, eh Jess?

144

[*She pats her.*]

MRS GREEN: Heaven rejoices at a sinner saved.

PASTOR: I hope you'll testify on Sunday, Jess.

JESS: I will.

PASTOR: Now let's lay your hands on Jess and ask the Lord's
blessing. Kneel down, Jess.

[JESS *kneels down and the others circle her, laying hands on her
shoulders and head.* JESS *keeps her eyes open and stares into*
PASTOR's *knees.*]

PASTOR: Oh Jesus, thank you for taking this sinner and passing
fire through her heart. Thank you for purging her body of its
lusts and passions. You have scraped clean her mind and torn
from her bowels the heat she feels for another. Smash her pride,
flay her with your love. May she bear the wounds of love Christ
Jesus, the bleeding wounds of love . . .

[DIALOGUE OVER PASTOR:

JESS: Will you write to me?

MELANIE: I can't. We've got to forget.

JESS: I won't forget.

MELANIE: I'll miss you.

JESS: You don't have to miss me. You could love me.

MELANIE: It's not simple anymore.

JESS: I love you.]

. . . Amen.

MOTHER/MRS GREEN/MAY: Amen. Praise the Lord. Amen.

THREE

EXT. FAIRGROUND. FANTASY. NIGHT

All the characters we've met are in dodgem cars riding round and round, laughing and shouting. SMALL JESS *and* JESS *share a car. Suddenly* MOTHER's *car bumps* JESS's, *then the others begin to do the same, herding her car round the ring. Even* MELANIE *does it. The cars close in, corralling* JESS. *It doesn't feel like a game anymore. The cars come to a halt entirely surrounding* JESS. *We see* JESS's *face, frightened and confused. She holds* SMALL JESS's *hand. When the camera goes back to the other cars, all the characters have put on flat doll-like masks and are leaning forward. The fairground music is still playing. Suddenly* JESS *gets up and, without looking back, walks across the bonnets of the cars and out of the ring.*

INT. GOSPEL TENT. BLACKPOOL. DAY

JESS *is on the platform.* PASTOR *is near by,* MAY *has her tambourine out and is wearing a banner which says: 'Seek ye the Lord while He may be found.' The tent is full of people.* PASTOR *comes forward to the rudimentary microphone.*

PASTOR: For our closing appeal, I'd like to bring somebody to you who has a special place in the hearts of all of us here.

[*He sweeps his arms about the platform to indicate the church rather than the flock.*]

She's been ill, she's been tempted, but she's come back to Jesus a hundredfold. Now if any of you doubt the love of Jesus, I want you to come up here after the service and talk to Jess.

[*The* PASTOR *stands back and makes room for* JESS. *The platform lot murmur their approval. Cut to* MOTHER *and* MRS GREEN *in the front row.*]

146

MRS GREEN: She's lost none of her gift.

MOTHER: It's my prayers and nursing.

[*Cut.* JESS *is standing in front of the microphone.* PASTOR *has sat down again.*]

JESS: Tonight, when you came into this tent, many of you had never heard of how Jesus died for your sins. He died so that you could live. He was bound so that you could be free. Anyone can know that love of Jesus and there is no sin so great that He cannot forgive it.

PASTOR: [*Loudly*] Amen, Amen.

JESS: Anyone can know his peace, you don't need brains or money, all you need to do is ask. If anyone wants to get closer to Jesus, don't wait, come up to the front now, so that we can pray with you. Come up now, and open your hearts to Jesus.

[*The piano starts to play 'He Touched Me' and two people stand up and make their way to the front.* JESS *and* PASTOR *go towards them. Suddenly a rather striking young girl of about sixteen* [KATY] *comes forward.* JESS *kneels down with her and they smile at each other.* PASTOR *comes and stands over them, his arms upraised in blessing.*]

INT. BOARDING HOUSE. BEDROOM. BLACKPOOL. NIGHT

A dingy boarding-house bedroom. MOTHER *is sitting up in bed with her curlers in, reading.* WILLIAM *lies next to her, asleep. The door opens slowly and* JESS *pokes her head round.*

MOTHER: I'm not asleep.

JESS: Sorry I'm late, it's all those new converts. There's still some left in the tent.

MOTHER: Well, go back then. It's what your training's for. And after your illness you need plenty of life with the Lord. I told you you'd be called to work once you got better.

JESS: What are you reading?

MOTHER: It's a book Pastor Spratt sent me. It's called 'Where White Man Fears To Tread'. It's all about the experiences of a missionary. You should borrow it.

JESS: Thanks, I will. I'll take a scarf with me if I'm going back outside.

[*She puts on a warmer jersey and a scarf, while* MOTHER *bangs on.*]

MOTHER: Did you know, they fed some white mice the same diet that Indians eat and all the mice died. It just goes to show how the Lord provides for Christian countries.

JESS: And you don't think the mice would have died if you'd fed them on steak and kidney pudding?

EXT. BLACKPOOL. DAY

PASTOR, MOTHER, MRS GREEN, MAY, JESS, KATY, *two men and a few others are on the pier having a picnic. Food is spread out. The two men are fiddling with their rods and lines, the church lot are singing a chorus: 'I will make you fishers of men.' As they come to the end, they stand up and clap and* PASTOR *raises his hands.*

PASTOR: It was Jesus's way to spend His time with simple ordinary people, like the fishermen of the sea of Galilee, like the crowd that came to listen and who He fed in their thousands with only five loaves and two fishes. Jesus went out of His way to meet people. That's why we come on these missions. We want to follow the example of Jesus. Whatever Jesus did, we want to do.

MAY: Amen, Amen.

FIRST MAN: Why don't you walk on the bloody water then?

PASTOR: What?

FIRST MAN: The water. Jesus walked on it, didn't he? You said you wanted to do the same things.

PASTOR: That was a miracle.

SECOND MAN: Have you ever thought that Jesus might have been a member of the Magic Circle, like Michael here? Michael saws people in half.

FIRST MAN: I think Jesus was a magician. All them miracles. He's got to be.

SECOND MAN: Got to be.

PASTOR: I'm going to lead the believers in a Word of Prayer on your behalf. On Judgement Day you'll be unhappy men. Hell is always close at hand for the scoffers and the hard-hearted.

[*He closes his eyes and lifts his head towards heaven.*]

PASTOR: Oh, Heavenly Father, shake up the world with Your love . . .

[*As he drones on* KATY *moves forward towards* JESS *and tugs at her sleeve.* JESS *opens her eyes.*]

PASTOR: [*Voice over*] Let us feel the shudders of your love from Blackpool to Bangkok. Let them sigh and heave the name of Jesus. Let it be You, Lord, they cry out for in the night. Let it be You they turn towards in the middle of the long and lonely night. Let it be Your name on their lips. Your hand on their hearts. May the very tips of their toes know the glory of the living God . . .

KATY: [*Whispering*] I don't understand. Will you explain everything to me?

JESS: Don't worry, it's hard getting used to being a Christian at first. You'll soon be all right.

KATY: Can we talk about it later?

JESS: I've got to go back to the boarding house with my mum but we could meet afterwards, after the service.

KATY: [*Nodding*] Which one's your mum?

[JESS *points to her* MOTHER's *substantial back view.*]

JESS: That one.

KATY: She's the one who never smiles.

JESS: She doesn't think it's right to smile when there are so many people going to Hell.

KATY: Oh.

JESS: Close your eyes now.

PASTOR: [*cont.*] . . . Amen, Amen, Amen, Amen, Sweet Jesus.

FIRST MAN: I'm not bothered about going to Hell. At least this bloody lot won't be there.

SECOND MAN: I wouldn't bank on it.

EXT. PROM. BLACKPOOL. NIGHT

JESS *and* KATY *are down on the prom leaning over the railing and looking into the water. The night is still lively.*

KATY: Mum doesn't believe in church. I liked your sermon

149

though. All that about love. [*She pauses.*] We can still have a
good time can't we? Now that we're saved.

JESS: Yes, you don't stop having a good time because you belong
to Jesus.

KATY: Let's go to the Pleasure Beach then.

JESS: I can't!

KATY: Why not?

JESS: Because I'm supposed to be talking to you about Jesus.

KATY: Can you only talk to me about Jesus standing still?

JESS: No, but . . .

KATY: Come on then. There's a tram. Let's run for it.

[*She sets off;* JESS *sprints behind her.*]

EXT. DODGEMS AND PLEASURE BEACH RIDES. BLACKPOOL. NIGHT

JESS *and* KATY *in a dodgem.*

KATY: Do you know about the Locomotion?

JESS: What?

KATY: The Locomotion. You drive, I want to dance.

[*The dodgems start up,* JESS *deeply taken aback,* KATY
bouncing up and down in her seat.]

[CUT TO: JESS *and* KATY *walk through the fair. They ride on the
Blue Elephants, play the Camel Game, ride the big dipper, ride
on the whip-cars.*]

EXT. MERRY-GO-ROUND. PLEASURE BEACH. BLACKPOOL. NIGHT

JESS *and* KATY *are sitting on adjacent horses shouting across at
each other.*

JESS: I love the fair. We have one near where I live every year. I
always go. They've got Fortune Tellers too. I had my fortune
told once.

[*Her words are drowned by a sudden blast of music.* KATY
*blows her a kiss and concentrates on the ride. A boy from
another horse leans across to her.* KATY *laughs and shakes her
head.*]

What did he say?

KATY: Nothing. I told him I was with you.

EXT. CARAVAN. BLACKPOOL. NIGHT

Very dark, very quiet, very late.

JESS and KATY are sitting side by side on the steps of a caravan.
They are lit by a tilly lamp.

JESS: Where do your Mum and Dad sleep.

KATY: They sleep in the boarding house. Me and my sister sleep in the caravan.

JESS: Will our talking wake her up?

KATY: No, she's not here tonight. She's with my grandma in Fleetwood. I'm going tomorrow night. She only likes us one at a time.

JESS: Was it good?

KATY: What?

JESS: Tonight.

KATY: You were there – was it good?

JESS: Yes. I haven't had so much fun in ages. I was ill and before that I was unhappy.

KATY: And now?

JESS: Well, I'm not ill and I'm happy.

[KATY *leans on* JESS.]

KATY: You were going to tell me about Jesus.

JESS: What was it that you wanted to know?

KATY: Well, I think you should teach me gradually.

[JESS *turns to look at her and says quite softly.*]

JESS: Well, not too much at once.

KATY: No, let's take a long time.

[JESS *breaks the moment by standing up so suddenly that* KATY *slips over.*]

JESS: I'm sorry. I forgot how late it was. I just heard the clock chime.

KATY: I didn't. Are you off then?

[JESS *looks at her.*]

JESS: Yeah.

KATY: Don't you want a cup of tea?

[JESS *shakes her head.*]

KATY: Well, good night then.

[*She steps forward towards* JESS *and gives her a hug. It's a very tight hug.* JESS *pulls back and looks at* KATY. *It's very close, face to face. Slowly* KATY *moves to kiss her;* JESS *hesitates then joins in. No hurry about this shot.*]

INT. PARLOUR. ELSIE'S HOUSE. DAY

JESS: I kept trying to see you but Pastor said you were too ill. Did you like my letters?

ELSIE: What letters? I never had any.

JESS: I gave them to Pastor. One each time he went to visit you. He said he'd give them to you but not to expect a reply because you were so weak.

ELSIE: I never saw them, love. And I wasn't that weak. Funny, when I asked him to fetch you down with him, he said you had Glandular Fever.

JESS: Oh, I did, but only for four months.

INT. BIRTWISTLE'S CAFE. DAY

JESS *is in the cafe in town doing the washing up.* MRS ARKWRIGHT *is serving through a little hatch.* JESS *is in an overall; she has the transistor on. It's playing The Supremes, 'Stop in the Name of Love'. Suddenly* MRS ARKWRIGHT *turns around.*

MRS ARKWRIGHT: Oy!

JESS: What?

MRS ARKWRIGHT: There's nipper out here to see you.

[JESS *smiles, wipes her hands and goes out to the front of the cafe where* KATY *is waiting.* JESS *and* KATY *leave the cafe.*]

EXT. MARKET. DAY

JESS: You're late today. I thought you weren't coming.

KATY: I had to get my brother ready for Cubs.

JESS: I'm sorry. It's just I'm fed-up because you're going back to school next week.

KATY: We'll still have our Saturdays and Sundays and we'll see each other most nights at church. Anyway, you'll be at Tech again soon.

JESS: Yeah, but I'll carry on working at the caff. Mrs Arkwright's given me a split shift for the weekdays.

KATY: You'll be tired.

JESS: Let's go in there.

[*She pulls* KATY *down a side alley stacked with boxes and market containers. They can make enough room for themselves and not be seen.* KATY *moves forward and kisses* JESS *on the neck and face.*]

JESS: Do I smell of milk shakes?

KATY: Pineapple.

[*She nuzzles deeper.*]

JESS: Oh, I wish we had somewhere proper to go – somewhere of our own.

KATY: We've got my mum's caravan. We can stay there whenever we want. You could come tonight if you want.

JESS: No, I can't. I've got to prepare a Bible study for the Harvest Festival.

KATY: We'll do that first and I'll type it for you. Then we can go to bed.

JESS: Don't you ever worry that we might be doing something wrong?

KATY: No.

[*She smiles at* JESS *and moves in for more kisses.*]

INT. CHURCH. DAY

MOTHER, MAY *and* MRS GREEN *are in their best clothes presiding over the Harvest Festival table packed with perishables and tins.* MOTHER *is putting the finishing touch to a huge pyramid of oranges.*

MOTHER: Where's William? He should be back by now. I had to send him home to get a clean tie.

MAY: Oh, here he comes, and Elsie with him. Oh, doesn't she look grand?

[WILLIAM *comes forward pushing* ELSIE *in a wheelchair. He's wearing a sober suit and a very flamboyant tie.* ELSIE *wears her fruit hat.*]

MOTHER: Ahhh, hello Mrs Norris. You're the first. Will you take your pick?

ELSIE: Harvest Festival. What a day!

[*She pauses, looking at the table.*]

There's a lot of tins this year aren't there?

MOTHER: Don't worry about that. William will carry them for you.

MAY: It's holocaust food.

ELSIE: What?

MOTHER: We're living in the last days, Mrs Norris, as well we know. At any moment the Lord may come back and the earth will be consumed by a fireball as it says in the Book of Revelation. These tins will tide us over while we wait in the bunker for the Lord's call. You can't count on perishables.

ELSIE: I see. Well, unless the holocaust comes pretty fast, I'm going to miss it, so why not give me whatever'll rot quickest and I'll go and and eat it right away.

MRS GREEN: Bread and cheese? We've got Cheshire or Lancashire crumbly.

MAY: Hey, I've got some cream cakes. Take those.

[*She offers a box to* ELSIE *who takes it and looks inside.*]

ELSIE: Chocolate eclairs and strawberry tarts. These'll do. Come on, William!

[*She calls him from where he is getting boxes ready to put the food in.*]

Push me to one side and I'll have a cup of tea and get stuck in. Champion!

[*She grins at* MAY.]

EXT. CHURCH STEPS. DAY

JESS *and* KATY *are on two step ladders fixing a huge basket of painted fruit over the church door.*

KATY: It looks like Elsie's hat.

JESS: Oh, yes. Pass me that hammer, will you? Thanks.

[KATY *passes it over.*]

Pastor's up to something.

KATY: How do you know?

JESS: I can tell by the way he's rubbing his hands and saying Praise the Lord. [*She pauses*] Right. Let's get down and have a look. It's got to be straight . . .

[*As* KATY *and* JESS *are admiring their handiwork, a motorbike pulls up. Not a flash motorbike, a horrible CZ. The man driving it is tall and lanky with round glasses. He wears an army surplus combat jacket and black army boots. The passenger takes off her helmet. It's* MELANIE.]

JESS: Oh God.

MELANIE: Hello Jess.

[*She gets off the bike and hugs her.* JESS *makes no move.* KATY *stands in the background. The boyfriend,* IAN, *gets off and starts tinkering with his bike.*]

I came early to find you because we've got to go off straight after the service to stay with Ian's parents up in Yorkshire. We're getting married, Jess.

[MELANIE's *beaming.* JESS *looks like she's been struck.*]

JESS: You never wrote to me. I wrote to you every week; you never answered.

MELANIE: Oh Jess don't. Be happy for me.

JESS: This is Katy.

[MELANIE's *smile freezes but she rallies.*]

MELANIE: Hello. Are you Jess's friend?

KATY: Yes, I was saved at the tent crusade. I know all about you.
[*She moves closer to* JESS.]

MELANIE: Well, I'd better go inside and have a word with your mum. What are you doing now?

JESS: Doing for what?

[MELANIE *blushes and turns towards the bike.*]

MELANIE: Ian, come and meet Jess.

[IAN *lumbers over and holds out his hand which* JESS *ignores.*]
And this is . . . I'm sorry, I've forgotten.

KATY: Katy. Pleased to meet you.

JESS: Come on Katy, let's go.

MELANIE: Are you not staying for the service?

JESS: Not if you are.

155

[*They turn to go. Suddenly* IAN *speaks.*]

IAN: Jess, as you know, Melanie's soon to be my wife. I want you to know that she's told me everything that went on between you . . .

JESS: Not everything.

IAN: Yes, everything, and I forgive you.

JESS: What?

IAN: I forgive you.

[MELANIE *is beaming away.* JESS *goes closer and looks up at him. Suddenly she spits right in his face and she and* KATY *turn away leaving* MELANIE *wiping him clean with her handkerchief.*]

EXT. GRAVEYARD. DAY

JESS *and* KATY *are sitting on a grave in the cemetery.* JESS *has her knees drawn up under her chin. She's crying.* KATY *is holding her.*

JESS: Can I come and stay with you? I can live in your caravan.

[KATY *is stroking her hair and holding her.*]

KATY: You can't. Mum wouldn't let you. She doesn't like you because of church. She thinks you've led me astray. She isn't keen on God.

JESS: I can't go home. Mum'll probably have Melanie there.

KATY: She won't. Why should she?

JESS: Oh because she's holy now. I don't want to see her. I never want to see her again.

INT. BATHROOM. DAY

MOTHER *is redecorating.* JESS *sits on the landing.*

MOTHER: To think I trusted you and let you do as you pleased and I've worked to be a good mother and this is how you repay me.

[PASTOR *crosses* JESS *on his way into bathroom.*]

I wouldn't have believed it if Melanie hadn't told me herself. And to think it was her I blamed once.

PASTOR: Shall we go downstairs and have a nice cup of tea?

MOTHER: There's no cups left. I've smashed them all. What are we going to do?

PASTOR: Jess, we've let you have too much power and taking the Bible study — you've been a leader and it's not given for a woman to be a leader. We let you have a man's role and you've taken on a man's appetites.

MOTHER: She's lost, she's lost.

PASTOR: She's in danger of losing her soul.

JESS: I'm fine.

[*She gets up and goes downstairs.*]

MOTHER: Where do you think you're going?

JESS: I don't know but I'm not going back in that parlour.

EXT. GRAVEYARD. DAY

JESS *running hell for leather through the churchyard. She almost collides with* CISSY *who grabs on to her.*

CISSY: Steady on girl! What's the trouble? There's nothing worth that pace.

JESS: I'm leaving home.

CISSY: What's happened?

JESS: It's Melanie. It's Katy. Mum hates me and the Pastor hates me, and the whole Council's turned against me. They think I want to be a man.

CISSY: Oh yes. I have a sense of what you're saying. Elsie's told me enough.

JESS: I don't know what to do.

CISSY: What about your mother?

JESS: I don't know. I don't know anything . I've got to warn Katy in case they hurt her.

CISSY: I'll have a word with Katy. Now you'll be best off at Elsie's than chasing all over town. You're taking your exams, aren't you?

[JESS *nods and wipes her nose.*]

And it's important to do well isn't it?

JESS: Yes. Yes.

CISSY: You've no money but you can drive.

JESS: Yes, the Pastor taught me so that I could help him drive the mini-bus on our crusades.

CISSY: Right. You come to me and do a bit of work for your keep. Ever made up a corpse?

[JESS *looks a bit shocked.*]

JESS: No.

CISSY: There's nothing to it and the best thing is they don't complain when you show 'em the mirror. We'll see how it goes and you can come and go as you please. I can get you other bits of jobs too. Moonlighting for Brimstone's Ice-cream – they're always on the lookout for new drivers. Oh here . . .

[*She gives* JESS *a hankerchief.* JESS *blows her nose vigorously.*] You'll see a lovely Death's Head in the corner of that hanky, I sew 'em myself and sell 'em to the grieving.

[JESS *looks in the corner and starts to smile through her misery.*] Now, you do what you have to do and I'll expect you when I see you.

MONTAGE:

INT. ELYSIUM FIELDS FUNERAL PARLOUR. DAY

JESS *unplugs ice-cream van from morgue.*

EXT. ELYSIUM FIELDS. DAY

JESS *driving van up hill.*

INT. ELYSIUM FIELDS. DAY

JESS *and* CISSY *are in the office of 'Elysium Fields' making* JESS *a bed and curtained area for her to sleep.*

INT. ELYSIUM FIELDS. DAY

CISSY, JESS *and* ELSIE *eating at the long table.*

INT. ELYSIUM FIELDS. DAY

CISSY *and* JESS *taking a pile of* JESS'S *books out of the hearse.*

INT. ELSIE'S HOUSE. DAY

JESS *tucking* ELSIE *into bed.*

EXT. ELYSIUM FIELDS. DAY

JESS *polishing the sign of 'Elysium Fields'.*

INT. JESS'S ROOM. ELYSIUM FIELDS. DAY

CISSY *and* JESS *arranging books on makeshift shelves of bricks and planks.*

EXT. GRAVEYARD. DAY

CISSY *and* JESS *are tidying up some of the older graves, cutting back bushes, etc. Suddenly* JESS *points to a hand sticking up out of one of the graves and screeches.*
JESS: Cissy, look!
   [CISSY *goes over and pulls it up – it's plastic.*]

INT. JESS'S ROOM. ELYSIUM FIELDS. NIGHT

JESS *in her little room above the funeral parlour studying her books late at night. Bugs Bunny is nearby on a shelf. She puts out the light.*

END MONTAGE

EXT. ELSIE'S HOUSE. DAY

JESS *parking the ice-cream van outside a terraced house. She jumps out with choc-ices and goes in through the door shouting to* ELSIE.

INT. PARLOUR. ELSIE'S HOUSE. DAY

JESS: Elsie! Elsie! I've brought . . . you a choc-ice.

[*Her voice trails off as she looks around the living room.* PASTOR, MAY *and* MRS GREEN *are there.* ELSIE *is lying under a sheet.*]

PASTOR: This is no place for you, Jess. You're not of the flock now.

JESS: But I've brought Elsie a choc-ice. I bring it to her every Saturday and Sunday, when I'm on the van.

MAY: She'll not be needing ice-cream in glory.

JESS: Is she dead?

PASTOR: Go home, Jess.

JESS: [*Angry*] And where do you think that is?

EXT. ELSIE'S HOUSE. DAY

JESS *rushes out of the door and is greeted by a milling crowd around the van.*

SECOND WOMAN: It's two wafers please, love.

FIRST WOMAN: Was she a friend of yours?

[JESS *is concentrating hard on the wafers.*]

JESS: Yes.

FIRST WOMAN: She went last night – I saw her at six and she were dead by eight.

SECOND WOMAN: It's shocking.

FIRST WOMAN: It is, it makes you think. No sauce on one please, love.

JESS: How did she die?

FIRST WOMAN: A stroke I heard. Nothing long-winded. She went like that.

[*She snaps her fingers and takes the wafers. As the women turn away,* MRS GREEN *pushes to the front of the queue.*]

MRS GREEN: You get away from here, plying your trade amongst the dead.

JESS: It's not holy is it?

MRS GREEN: No it isn't but you'll pay for it and it'll be more than the cost of a cornet.

[*She turns away sobbing.* JESS *ignores the rest of the queue and drives away. A little way down the road she slows to a halt, bangs on the steering wheel and shouts, 'No,' with all the pain of a wounded animal.*]

EXT. ELYSIUM FIELDS. DAY

JESS *is sitting with* CISSY *in the back of the hearse.* CISSY *is making a wreath. A pot of tea and a packet of bourbons lie between them.*

CISSY: Have a bourbon. Best thing to come out of France.

JESS: And what about quiche?

CISSY: Oh yes, quiche. I had some of that the other day from that posh new shop. I think I might put it on the menu for funeral lunches. It'll make a change from turkey roll. Have you ever been to France?

JESS: No. Have you?

CISSY: No, wouldn't want to neither. Some are cut out for travel and others it is who stay at home. How are you getting on with that ice-cream van job?

JESS: Oh, all right. It's better for me to be working. That way I've no time to get upset.

[CISSY *pats her hand and pours more tea.*]

CISSY: Do us a favour tonight. I want to go and see that old Gary Cooper film and I've got the vehicle to sweep out for tomorrow. Will you do it for me and give it a good clean?

JESS: It's for Elsie, isn't it?

CISSY: It is. It's full of earth in the back though from where our undertaker used it for fetching the veg. from the allotment. It needs a good sweep. There's enough earth where she's going.

[JESS *goes over to the hearse and looks inside.*]

JESS: I'll do it.

CISSY: You're a good 'un. They won't let you go to the funeral will they?

JESS: No.

CISSY: Well, she'll be in the Chapel of Rest tonight, I shouldn't but I'll give you the key if you want to pay your respects.
[JESS *smiles*.]

EXT. ELYSIUM FIELDS. NIGHT

Night is falling. JESS *is polishing the hearse with a wash leather. She finishes and unlocks the Chapel of Rest.*

INT. CHAPEL OF REST. NIGHT

ELSIE's *coffin is surrounded by candles. It's resting at about waist height so* JESS *can easily see inside. She goes over and strokes* ELSIE's *forehead, then takes from her own neck a cross and chain and puts it on* ELSIE.

JESS: You can bear this better than I can.
[*She takes a stool and sits down.*]
There's so much I haven't told you because there's so much I haven't done yet. Who's going to listen to me now? Who's going to help me win a prize? I'm going to sit an entrance exam because I've read of this magical city full of towers and books where you can spend three years in a library. Just think of that, Elsie, how many books I can read. I'm not telling anyone except you and Cissy because it might never happen. I don't know if they accept people from Lancashire. But I've got to get away now. Everything that matters has gone. You, Mum and Dad, Melanie, God, the church. And I had to leave Katy to make it all right for her. I hope there is another world. I hope I'm brave.
[*The candles begin to burn down.* JESS *gets up and takes a winding sheet out of the cupboard, wraps herself in it and lies down on the floor under* ELSIE's *coffin.*]
I won't leave you tonight Elsie.
[*She sleeps.*]

INT. CHAPEL OF REST. DAY

Light fills the chapel. It is early morning and a telephone is ringing. JESS *stumbles awake and goes through into the office.*

JESS: Hello? Elysium Fields.

CISSY: Jess, it's me, Cissy. Did I get you out of bed?

JESS: No – yes, but it's all right.

CISSY: That's the trouble with living over the shop. Now listen, we're in bother. My helper can't come in today, I know it's supposed to be your day off, but I need you to help me with the cooking and the serving.

JESS: Cissy, I can't. It's Elsie's day today, the whole church will be at the meal. I can't do it.

CISSY: Don't panic. I'll keep you in the kitchen. Nobody'll see you. You can't let me down – it's turkey roll for twenty.

INT. DINING ROOM AND KITCHEN. ELYSIUM FIELDS. DAY

A long table is set for twenty. PASTOR, MAY, MRS GREEN, MOTHER *and* WILLIAM *and* MRS ARKWRIGHT *are sitting next to each other. The rest of the places are filled with people we don't know. They are all eating turkey roll;* CISSY *is clearing plates. She goes into the steaming kitchen where* JESS *is washing pans.*

CISSY: A woman of my training waiting on tables – it's not right.
[*The phone rings.* CISSY *answers it.*]

CISSY: You what? You're joking? Have you tried fire-lighters? We've got two to manage this afternoon and they're banked up tomorrow, we've got to get it lit. No I can't come over, I've got a wake going on. They haven't had their ice-cream yet. No. No! Oh, all right, I'll fetch some petrol.
[*She bangs down the telephone.*]
Jess, we're in crisis. There's a cremation in half an hour and they can't get the furnace to light. I've got to go over there.

JESS: No!

CISSY: Yes! When folk are dead you can't have 'em lying about. What about my professional pride? I've got to get them bodies burnt. Oh, I hate cremating. Why can't they go in the ground like they're supposed to?

JESS: But I'll have to do the ice-cream. They won't come to you anymore if they see me.

CISSY: I don't care. There's no shortage of bodies, and if they don't like my establishment they can go to Gloomy Alf's.
[*She marches off.*
JESS *picks up one of the trays and, walking behind the row of seated guests, starts plonking down the vanilla in front of them.*
MRS GREEN *turns in her seat and gives a little cry.*]

MRS GREEN: The Lord save us, it's Satan's limb.

PASTOR: You!

JESS: Me. Vanilla, Pastor?

MRS ARKWRIGHT: 'Ello. Give us a big one.

MAY: Have you no shame?

JESS: No.

PASTOR: We'll not stay here to be insulted.
[*They all get up except* MRS ARKWRIGHT *who eats eagerly.*]

MRS GREEN: She is a demon, your daughter.

MOTHER: No daughter of mine.
[*They troop out of the hall.* JESS *puts the tray down on the table and walks into the kitchen. The relatives look alarmed but don't do anything.* MRS ARKWRIGHT *takes another dish of ice-cream.*
Cut. In the kitchen, JESS *is holding on to the sink and fighting back her tears. A hand touches her shoulder.* JESS *turns around — it's* MISS JEWSBURY.]

JESS: I didn't see you in there.

MISS JEWSBURY: I was at the funeral but I didn't want to eat. I was hoping I'd see you. Elsie told me that you'd left home and left the church. She said you're driving an ice-cream van and making up corpses for Cissy.
[JESS *wipes her eyes and laughs.*]

JESS: I am. I'm at the Tech too working hard and trying for a place at University. I want to read a lot more books than the Bible.

MISS JEWSBURY: Is there anything I can do? Do you want my address?

JESS: No. I've got used to being on my own now.

MISS JEWSBURY: Well then. I'll be going. You can always find me in the phone book if you change your mind. Goodbye Jess. Remember you have to fight for what you want.
[*She goes out. Short shot of* JESS's *face.*]

INT. SCHOOL HALL. DAY

A large hall full of desks set in rows for an examination. There's a huge clock on the wall. Some young people are already at their desks. JESS *goes to the front and speaks quietly and nervously to the supervisor who should be rather forbidding.*

JESS: I've come to sit the entrance exam for Oxford.

[*The* WOMAN *nods, looks for some papers and leads* JESS *to a desk.*]

INT. SCHOOL HALL. DAY

Later. Shot of JESS *writing furiously and glancing at the clock.*

INT. HEARSE. DAY

JESS *is driving with* CISSY *next to her.*

CISSY: When will you find out then?

JESS: Soon. I've got an interview next week.

CISSY: I didn't know you were clever.

JESS: I might not be.

CISSY: Still, you've got a good heart.

JESS: You sound just like my mum.

CISSY: What do you mean?

JESS: She used to say, whenever I had exams or wanted to stay off church to revise, 'The test is how you live your life'.

CISSY: [*Laughing*] She's right too.

JESS: Yeah, I know that but it's very hard to live your life when everything you love has been taken away from you.

CISSY: Why don't you make it up with her?

JESS: I can't. She won't make it up with me. I'm not what she wants. I'm not what she intended. I've gone a different way.

CISSY: Time's a great healer.

INT. ELYSIUM FIELDS. DAY

JESS *is making up a corpse on the table. She has the radio on.* CISSY *rushes in holding a letter.*

CISSY: It's here.

JESS: What?

[*She doesn't turn for a second then suddenly she realises what* CISSY *means. She turns.*]

JESS: Oh no, I can't look.

CISSY: Shall I look?

JESS: No – yes – oh no, give it here. I will.

[CISSY *hands over the letter and pops a look at* JESS's *corpse.*]

CISSY: Oh, you've given her a lovely colour. She was never that good looking in life. They used to call her the Dust Pan.

JESS: I'm shaking.

CISSY: I know how you feel. When I got the telegram during the war, I thought, either me husband's been decorated or he's dead. Oh, it was such a relief when he were dead.

[JESS *rips open the letter with one of the make-up tools and scans the contents. Her face breaks with joy. She leaps around and hugs* CISSY.]

EXT. SWEETSHOP. DAY

JESS *running up the street towards the hill as in Episode One. She rushes into the sweetshop where the two women still are, but older.*

JESS: I'm going to Oxford.

[*She runs out of the sweetshop and keeps going towards the hill – over this her voice is repeating,* 'I'm going to Oxford'.]

EXT. HILLTOP. DAY

JESS *looking back on the town.*

JESS: I'm going to Oxford.

EXT. TOWN. DAY

Underneath a huge Christmas tree in the town square. The Salvation Army are setting up their band on one side of the tree. JESS *comes by and stands to watch. Then, on the other side of the tree, she sees* MOTHER, PASTOR, WILLIAM, MAY, MRS GREEN *and* KATY *also setting up their instruments.* MOTHER *has a harmonium,* MAY, *a huge tambourine and a pair of giant castanets,* GRAHAM, *a guitar,* PASTOR, *a pair of stand-up bongos,* MRS GREEN, *a pair of cymbals and* KATY, *a trumpet.*

MOTHER: I don't know how we're to compete with all that brasswork.

MRS GREEN: Trust in the Lord. Didn't Joshua bring down the walls of Jericho just by blowing his own trumpet?

KATY: I'm not very good, Mrs Green. I've only had six lessons.

MAY: Oh, don't bother about that. I haven't had any.

[*She laughs and flourishes her tambourine.*]

PASTOR: Have we all got our instruments ready? I see the Salvation Army have got out their sheet music.

KATY: William hasn't got anything.

[*Everybody looks at* WILLIAM *who smiles sheepishly and, fishing in his pocket, brings out a comb and paper.*]

MOTHER: He's quiet but he's deep.

MRS GREEN: Shall we tender the olive branch just once more?

PASTOR: You mean ask if we can join forces?

MRS GREEN: Yes, for the Glory of God.

MAY: What, after what they said to me? And how they treated me?

PASTOR: Go on then, Katy. Go and ask the General if he'd like our support. If not, ask him which carol they mean to start with and we'll play something different.

KATY: Do I have to?

PASTOR: Yes.

MOTHER: I'll play on the harmonium to give you support. When they hear the notes of Jesus their hearts'll soften. Go on. What a moment!

[*She starts playing crooning chords on the harmonium.*
KATY *pushes her way towards the other side of the tree and is waylaid by* JESS.]

JESS: Katy, Katy.

[*It's an emotional moment. They laugh and hug.*]

KATY: I don't know why I'm hugging you after you abandoned me.

JESS: I had to, you know I did.

KATY: My parents are going out tonight. Why don't you come round?

JESS: Shall I?

KATY: Come late though. I have to go now, I'm offering terms of surrender to the General.

[*Salvation Army starts up: 'Come All Ye Faithful'.*]

JESS: What's going on? We always play with the Salvation Army at Christmas.

KATY: They upset May in the rehearsals. They told her she couldn't play her drum. May said it tells us in the Bible to make a joyful noise but the General said that's not the same thing as a bloomin' racket.

[*She slips away.* JESS *stands watching.* MRS ARKWRIGHT *comes up behind her.*]

MRS ARKWRIGHT: Hello, nipper. Merry Christmas. I'm just on my way home. Do you want to come and have a drink? You're old enough now.

JESS: Yeah, all right. Just hang on a minute, let me hear this.

MRS ARKWRIGHT: What?

[MRS GREEN *starts crashing away.* JESS *is laughing. She and* MRS ARKWRIGHT *move off.*]

EXT. GRAVEYARD. NIGHT

Light fading fast. JESS *is standing by* ELSIE's *grave arranging some holly and copper beech leaves in the vase. She sees some Christmas roses on another grave and nips over to steal them and put them on* ELSIE's. *As she does so she hears* CISSY *behind her.*

CISSY: Still thieving from them that can't catch you?

JESS: Only the best for Elsie.

CISSY: Are you coming back with me? I've just laid out the last one and put 'em on cold till after Christmas.

JESS: Not yet. I'm going to go and see Mum and Dad.

CISSY: [*Surprised*] That's news.

JESS: They were in the market place today. Nothing has changed but I thought, if I could accept them, then maybe they could just about accept me.

CISSY: I'll expect you when I see you then.

JESS: Do you think it'll be all right?
CISSY: I don't know, but you had to do it sometime.

EXT. JESS'S HOME. NIGHT

It's now completely dark. JESS *stands outside her own front door. The lights are on in the parlour. She hears music. It's 'Hark the Herald Angels Sing', but with a swing rhythm.* JESS *opens the front door and goes in.*

INT. PARLOUR. NIGHT

JESS *enters the parlour.* MOTHER *is sitting in front of a three-keyboard electronic organ. It must be dramatic and vulgar with plenty of knobs.* MOTHER *swivels round in her matching stool.*
MOTHER: Jess! Come and look at this. I can play 'In The Bleak Mid-winter' with or without tremolo. I've got a lovely percussion.
[*She demonstrates while she's talking.*]
Oh yes, I got rid of the piano soon after you left. Didn't want to play anymore. But then, after a bit, your father went out and came back with this. I wouldn't touch it at first. Wouldn't even dust it, but then, I thought, well I should, for his sake. He missed you, Jess.
JESS: I've got a place at Oxford.
MOTHER: I told the Pastor, I said, she'll come back to the Lord one day, it's only a matter of time. I'll pray her back.
JESS: Can I have a cup of tea?
MOTHER: You always were impatient.

INT. KITCHEN. NIGHT

They go into the kitchen. MOTHER *bangs on the kettle.*
JESS: Are you going to play at The Morecambe Guest House for the Bereaved this year?
MOTHER: Don't talk to me about that guest house. First it was Cissy betraying me and looking after you . . .
JESS: Mum . . .

MOTHER: Stop interrupting. First it was Cissy, then I found that they'd been having seances in the Billiard Room. Seances! Cavorting with the dead and advertising in the *Psychic News*. They called it a 'spiritual service'. I know what I call it. Devil Worship I call it. Anyway, I wrote a long piece about it for *The Band of Hope Review*. And then that Reverend Eli Bone who used to do all the prayer and love and be so holy. We found out that his wife's not his wife at all. It's his pompadour.

JESS: His what?

MOTHER: His pompadour. He's been living in sin with his pompadour.

[*The kettle starts whistling;* MOTHER *brews the tea.*]

JESS: Vengeance is mine saith the Lord.

MOTHER: I'm glad to see you still think of the Bible – perhaps you're not all lost. Anyway, you know me Jess. I always turn the other cheek but there's only so many cheeks in a day.

JESS: So are you not with the society anymore?

MOTHER: There is no society, I disbanded it.

JESS: Does Pastor Spratt know?

MOTHER: He told me to do as I thought right. Would you like a Royal Scot?

[*She gets out the biscuit tin.*]

MOTHER: Anyway, I've had my consolations. It's not only the organ that's electronic.

JESS: What do you mean?

MOTHER: Wait and see.

JESS: Where's the dog?

MOTHER: Dead.

[*She swigs her tea and looks mournful.*]

INT. LIVING ROOM. NIGHT

Later. The trimmings are all up. The tree is resplendent. A fire blazes in the hearth and there is a hostess trolley laden with pineapple dishes. Every conceivable kind of thing that can be made out of pineapple, MOTHER *has made. A baize card table is unfolded in front of the fire.* MOTHER, MRS GREEN, MAY *and* WILLIAM *sit around it. At this moment the sitting room door bursts open and a Father Christmas figure comes in with a sack on his back.*

PASTOR: Yo ho ho, Merry Christmas one and all in Jesus.

MAY: Who are you?

MRS GREEN: It's Father Christmas.

MAY: I know that, but who is it?

PASTOR: I bring you tidings of great joy and a present each.

[*He starts fumbling in his sack and hands out presents.* JESS *doesn't get one. He looks at her and throws back his hood.*]

PASTOR: Merry Christmas, Jess.

[JESS *says nothing.* MOTHER *comes forward.*]

MOTHER: She's just visiting, Pastor. Have a glass of lemonade. Would you like a party pie?

MAY: I'd never have guessed, you look so real.

MOTHER: I didn't expect you tonight, Pastor. I thought you were with the sick.

PASTOR: I am, Mrs Debden.

[*He leans forward and tries to stroke* JESS'*s hair. She backs off.* MOTHER *gives him his lemonade and a party pie. Now his hands are full.*]

MOTHER: I hope you'll stay with us till midnight and we'll all give thanks and wish Jesus Happy Birthday. I love Christmas.

PASTOR: Amen, Amen.

[*Cut to the clock striking twelve. General chorus of* 'Merry Christmas'.]

MOTHER: Christmas Day! Merry Christmas!

[JESS *watches them open their presents.* MOTHER *has dived under the tree and is ripping hers open.* WILLIAM *very carefully unwraps one of his two presents.* MRS GREEN *is shaking a tube-like apparatus to guess what it is.* MAY *has a book of exercises for the mature woman.* MOTHER *waves a catapult in the air and gives* DAD *a kiss.*]

MOTHER: This'll keep the cats off the roses. Oh, William.

[*We should be very conscious of* JESS *observing and not participating. As far as we can see, she has no presents. The scene is far away for her. Suddenly it becomes very vivid.*]

I'll open the rest in a minute. It's time for my broadcast now. Mrs Green, May, will you switch me on please?

[MRS GREEN *and* MAY *whip off the cover of a huge CB radio hiding in the corner of the room.*]

JESS: My God.

MOTHER: He used to be, and I pray he'll be so again. I told you I'd gone all electronic. I built it myself with an instruction book. That old bakelite thing blew up, so what could I do?

JESS: You could have bought an ordinary radio.

MOTHER: Times change, Jess.

MAY: But God changes not.

WILLIAM: Amen!

[*They all look at him in astonishment.*]

MOTHER: Jesus led me to this CB radio and now I broadcast regularly to electronic believers all over the North West. I've got quite a club going.

MAY: She's marvellous, your mother. You should be thankful.

JESS: I don't know what to say.

PASTOR: Ah, see how the Lord strikes the Heathen dumb.

MRS GREEN: You should give up the Devil and come home.

JESS: Merry Christmas, Mrs Green.

MRS GREEN: Merry Christmas, Jess.

JESS: Merry Christmas, May.

MAY: Oh, Merry Christmas, love.

JESS: Merry Christmas, Dad. [*She kisses him*] Merry Christmas, Mum.

[MOTHER *ignores her as she works her radio.* JESS *has put on her coat. She stands outside of the group who are now taken up with the humming CB.* MRS GREEN, MAY *and* WILLIAM *stand behind* MOTHER, PASTOR *is a little to the side by the Christmas tree.*]

PASTOR: May the airwaves be filled with the name of Jesus. Oh Lord, jam every other station but your own.

MRS GREEN/MAY: Amen, Praise the Lord.

MOTHER: Amen, Amen. Now, pass me my headphones.

[WILLIAM *passes them to her.* JESS *opens the door and stands a moment, watching.*]

I can feel the Spirit right through the North West. This is Kindly Light calling Manchester. Come in Manchester, this is Kindly Light.

[*Close on* JESS's *face and the sound of her voice.*]

JESS: [*Voice over*] Like most people I lived for a long time with my mother and father. My father liked to watch the wrestling, my mother liked to wrestle.